Ruby

P H R A S E B O O K

ESSENTIAL CODE AND COMMANDS

Jason Clinton

Addison-Wesley

Upper Saddle River, NJ • Boston • Indianapolis • San Francisco
New York • Toronto • Montreal • London • Munich • Paris • Madrid
Cape Town • Sydney • Tokyo • Singapore • Mexico City

Ruby Phrasebook

Copyright © 2009 by Pearson Education, Inc.

ISBN-13: 978-0-672-32897-8
ISBN-10: 0-672-32897-6
Library of Congress Cataloging-in-Publication Data:
2005938020
Printed in the United States of America
First Printing August 2008

Trademarks

All terms mentioned in this book that are known to be trademarks or service marks have been appropriately capitalized. Pearson Education, Inc. cannot attest to the accuracy of this information. Use of a term in this book should not be regarded as affecting the validity of any trademark or service mark.

Warning and Disclaimer

Every effort has been made to make this book as complete and as accurate as possible, but no warranty or fitness is implied. The information provided is on an "as is" basis. The author and the publisher shall have neither liability nor responsibility to any person or entity with respect to any loss or damages arising from the information contained in this book.

Bulk Sales

Pearson Education, Inc. offers excellent discounts on this book when ordered in quantity for bulk purchases or special sales. For more information, please contact

U.S. Corporate and Government Sales
1-800-382-3419
corpsales@pearsontechgroup.com

For sales outside of the U.S., please contact

International Sales
international@pearson.com

Editor-in-Chief
Mark Taub

Development Editor
Michael Thurston

Managing Editor
Patrick Kanouse

Project Editor
Jennifer Gallant

Copy Editor
Geneil Breeze/
Krista Hansing

Indexer
Tim Wright

Proofreader
Carla Lewis/
Leslie Joseph

Technical Editor
Robert Evans

Publishing Coordinator
Vanessa Evans

Multimedia Developer
Dan Scherf

Book Designer
Gary Adair

QA 76.41. Cas 2008

ecord in MARC
ord
efault Constant Data
Holdings
All Headings
ord
Editing
ster Record

Record Lock
t Record
cord
nstant Data Record
Holdings
Record
ave File Record
Constant Data Record

Table of Contents

About the Author

Jason Clinton has been working in the computer industry for more than a decade. He is actively involved in the Kansas City Ruby Users Group (KCRUG), serving as administrator of the group's website and mailing list, and he teaches a community class on Linux at University of Missouri-Kansas City.

Clinton uses Ruby daily in system administration and development for Advanced Clustering Technologies, a Linux Beowulf cluster integrator.

Acknowledgments

Without the Pragmatic Programmers' freely available first edition of *Programming Ruby*, I would have never discovered the wonderful world of Ruby. The Pickaxe books and the great Ruby community make projects like this one possible.

Thanks to my loving partner, Brandon S. Ward, for his infinite patience while I was working on this book.

We Want to Hear from You!

As the reader of this book, *you* are our most important critic and commentator. We value your opinion and want to know what we're doing right, what we could do better, what areas you'd like to see us publish in, and any other words of wisdom you're willing to pass our way.

You can email or write me directly to let me know what you did or didn't like about this book—as well as what we can do to make our books stronger.

Please note that I cannot help you with technical problems related to the topic of this book, and that due to the high volume of mail I receive, I might not be able to reply to every message.

When you write, please be sure to include this book's title and author as well as your name and phone number or email address. I will carefully review your comments and share them with the author and editors who worked on the book.

Email: feedback@developers-library.info

Mail: Mark Taber
           Pearson Education, Inc.
           800 East 96th Street
           Indianapolis, IN 46240 USA

Reader Services

Visit our website and register this book at informit.com/register for convenient access to any updates, downloads, or errata that might be available for this book.

Introduction

Audience

You can find some great Ruby books on the market. If you are new to Ruby, a friend or someone on the Internet has probably already listed some favorite Ruby books—and you *should* buy those books. But every book has its niche: Each attempts to appeal to a certain need of a programmer.

It is my belief that the best thing this book can do for you is *show you the code*. I promise to keep the chat to a minimum, to focus instead on the quality and quantity of actual Ruby code. I'll also keep as much useful information in as tight a space as is possible.

Unlike any other book on the market at the time of this writing, this book is intended to be a (laptop-bag) "pocket-size" resource that enables you to quickly look up a topic and find examples of practical Ruby code—a topical quick reference, if you will. In each of the topics covered, I try to provide as thorough an approach to each task as the size allows for; there's not as much room for coverage of topical solutions as there is in much larger books with similar goals, such as *The Ruby Way, 2nd Edition* (Sams, 2006), by Hal Fulton. Because of this, other issues that are often given equal priority are relegated to second. For instance, this is not a tutorial; the code samples have some explanation, but I assume that you have a passing familiarity with the language. Also, when possible, I try to point out issues related to security and performance, but I make no claim that these are my highest priority.

I hope that you find this book a useful tool that you keep next to your keyboard whenever you are *phrase-mongering* in Ruby.

How to Use This Book

I have not intended for this book to be read cover to cover. Instead, you should place your bookmark at the Table of Contents so you can open the book, find the topic you are programming on at the moment, and go immediately to a description of all the issues you might run into.

The content in the book is arranged by topic instead of Ruby class. The benefit is that you can go to one place in this book instead of four or five areas in Ruby's own documentation. (Not that there's anything wrong with Ruby's documentation. It's just that sometimes you are working with several classes at a time and, because Ruby's docs are arranged by class, you have to jump around a lot.)

Conventions

Phrases throughout the book are put in dark gray boxes at the beginning of every topic.

```
Phrases look like this.
```

Code snippets that appear in normal text are in *italics*. All other code blocks, samples, and output appear as follows:

```
# code sample boxes.
```

Parentheses are optional in Ruby in some cases—the rule is: you must have parentheses in your method call *if* you are calling another function in your list of parameters, or passing a literal code block to the method. In all other cases, parentheses are optional. Personally, I'm a sucker for consistency but one of the indisputable strengths of Ruby is the flexibility of the syntax.

In an attempt to have consistency between this book and others, I will (reluctantly) use `.class_method()` to refer to class methods, `::class_variable` to refer to class variables, `#method()` to refer to instance methods, and finally `#var` to refer to instance variables. When referring to variables and methods which are members of the *same* class, I'll use the appropriate `@variable` and `@@class_varriable`.

I know that some people might find these two rules annoying—especially those coming from languages that use the ':::' and '.' notation everywhere. In all practicality, you will never be so consistent—and rightfully so. One of Ruby's strengths is that there is a ton of flexibility. In fact, this flexibility has helped make Ruby on Rails so popular. This allowed the creators of Rails to make what appears to be a *domain-specific language* (a language well-suited for a specific kind of work) for web development. But really, all that is going on is a variation on Ruby syntax. And this is one of the many reasons that Ruby is more suitable for a given problem than, say, Python. Python's rigidity ("there should be

one—and preferably only one—obvious way to do it")
doesn't lend itself to DSL, so the programmers in that
language are forced to use other means (which might
or might not turn out to be unpleasant).

I always use single quotes (') in Ruby code *unless* I
actually want to make use of the double-quote (")
features (interpolation and substitution).

I always put the result of the evaluation of the statement (or block) on the next line with a proceeding
#=>, similar to what you would find if you were using
irb or browsing Ruby's documentation.

Comments on executable lines of code start with # and
are in *italics* to the end of the comment. Comments on
#=> lines are in parentheses and are in *italics*.

Acknowledgments

Without the Pragmatic Programmers' freely available
1st Edition of *Programming Ruby*, I would have never
discovered the wonderful world of Ruby. The Pickaxe
books and the great Ruby community are what make
projects like this one possible.

Thanks to my loving partner, Brandon S. Ward, for his
infinite patience while working on this book.

Reporting Errata

Readers will almost certainly find topics that they wish
were covered which we were overlooked when plan-
ning this book. I encourage you to please contact us
and let us know what you would like to see included
in later editions. Criticisms are also welcome. Contact
information can be found in the front-matter of this
book.

Converting Between Types

The word "type" comes with a lot of baggage and I use it deliberately here. Programmers coming from other languages will likely expect Ruby, like all languages, to implement certain core "types": integers, floats, strings, characters, etc. However, in Ruby there really isn't such a thing as a traditional primitive type. Even integers are stored as instances of the Fixnum (or Bignum) class. They are objects just like any other. If you are new to Ruby, you should keep repeating this to yourself as you are coding: "everything is an object, everything is an object, ...". That's the rule to swim or sink by in Ruby. Absolutely everything around is an object: an instance of a class.

Also, keep in mind that the rigidness that comes with statically typed languages is relaxed. Methods (generally) do not check to see whether an object that they are working with is an instance of a particular class. For example, the #puts method will accept any object which responds to a #to_s method call. So, if your object implements #to_s, you can use #puts. This is called "duck typing" – you'll see more discussion about this throughout the book.

Number from a String

```
'123'.to_i
    #=> 123
'123'.to_f
    #=> 123.0
```

String.to_i scans the literal value of the object and returns the value as an Integer. String.to_f scans the literal value of the object and returns the value as a Float. If you want the input to decide whether it gets stored as a Float or Fixnum, do this instead:

```
class String
    def to_real
        if self.include? '.'
            self.to_f
        else
            self.to_i
        end
    end
end

'123'.to_real
    #=> 123
'123.0'.to_real
    #=> 123.0
'1.23e10'.to_real
    #=> 12300000000.0
```

Number to Formatted String

```
123.to_s
    #=> "123"
(123.0).to_s
    #=> "123.0"
```

Often a simple conversion from **Integer** or **Float** to **String** will do—as in above.

However, Ruby also has the **sprintf** style of **String** formatting built in. C programmers will be familiar with this. Many **String** formatting codes exist; I cover just the numeric ones here in Table 1.1; refer to Table 2.1 for an additional list of the escape codes that can be used for formatting Strings. Also try **man sprintf** or **ri Kernel.sprintf** from a terminal on your favorite*nix (or Cygwin on Windows) for complete documentation of this feature.

Here are some examples of using **sprintf()**:

```
'The price is: %10d' % 123
    #=> "The price is:        123" (space padding)
'The price is: %10.2f' % 123
    #=> "The price is:     123.00"
'Hex Dump: %08x' % 1234567
    #=> "Hex Dump: 0012d687" (zero padding)
'Bin Dump: %08b' % 123
    #=> "Bin Dump: 01111011"
```

Print the hexadecimal code for each byte in the **String** "test":

```
'test'.each_byte do |byte|
    puts '%02x' % byteend
```

Sample output:

74
65
73
74

Use % to start an escape sequence and one of the values from the Code column to end the escape sequence. Everything between is the arguments.

Table 1.1   Numeric SprintF Codes

Numeric Code	Arguments Allowed	Explanation
D, i, or u	space, +, -, 0, *d	Integer argument is converted to decimal notation. d and i are synonyms. u forces unsigned interpretation.
X or X	space, #, +, -, 0, *d	Integer argument is converted to hex notation. d forces uppercase A to F.
o	space, #, +, -, 0, *d	Integer argument is converted to octal notation.
b	space, #, +, -, 0, *d	Integer argument is converted to binary notation.
f	d.d, space, #, +, -, 0, *d	Float argument is converted to floating notation with a leading zero before numbers less than 1 or greater than -1.

Numeric Code	Arguments Allowed	Explanation
e or E	d.d, space, #, +, -, 0, *d	Float argument is converted using f rules but with added exponent notation. E forces uppercase E.
g or G	d.d, space, #, +, -, 0, *d	Float argument is converted using f rules, but with added exponent notation only if the exponent is less than -4 or greater than or equal to the precision. G forces uppercase E.

unknown author, *printf man page*, 2000

Table 1.2 gives an explanation of what each of these arguments does.

Table 1.2 **Numeric SprintF Arguments**

Argument	Explanation
d.d	The first d is the width, the last d is an integer representing the precision of the floating point rendering. A - preceding this argument causes left justification.
space	Pad width with spaces.
#	Use alternate notation for hex, octal, and binary.
+	Always indicate sign.
-	Left justification.

Table 1.2   **Continued**

Argument	Explanation
0	Pad with zeros.
*d	d must be an integer indicating the width of the numerical representation.

Note that * is assumed for the first nonzero number encountered in the argument list.

String **to** Array **and Back Again**

```
'foobar'[3,1]
    #=> "b" (single character String)
'foobar'[3,2]
    #=> "ba"
'foobar and ruby'[-4,4]
    #=> "ruby"
'foobar'[2..5]   # (Ranges too! See below.)
    #=> "obar"
'foobar and ruby'[-4..-1]
    #=> "ruby"
'foobar'[2...5]
    #=> "oba"
'foobar and ruby'[-4...-1]
    #=> "rub"
```

As in many programming languages, a **String** object is merely an array of characters; internally, the actual **String** value is stored in a C-style array. Not surprisingly, then, ranges within **Strings** can be accessed by analogs to most of the usual **Array** operations. Refer to Table 1.3 for a list of ranges that can be used inside **String.[]**.

Here are some results that you might not expect at first glance:

```
'foobar'[4]
   #=> 97 (this is the ASCII value of 'a')
'foobar'[4,0]
   #=> "" (a null string)
'foobar'[4..200]
   #=> "ar" (no out of range error)
```

Table 1.3   String Slicing Operators

String Ranges	Positions (Counting starts at 0, Negative Numbers Count Position from the End)
S[{start}..{end}]	{start} includes the character; {end} includes the character.
S[{start}...{end}]	{start} includes the character; {end} excludes the character.
S[{start}, {count}]	{start} includes the character; {count} positions from start to include. Use 1 to get a one-character string.

You can also assemble a String from an Array of Strings:

```
['this','is','a','test'].join ' '
   #=> "this is a test"
```

Also see the subsection "Replacing Substrings" in "Working with Strings" for information about replacing parts of Strings using slicing operators.

String **to Regular Expression and Back Again**

```
Regexp.new 'mystring'
    #=> /mystring/
Regexp.new '\d{4}-\d{2}-\d{2}'
    #=> /\d{4}-\d{2}-\d{2}/

/\d\d:\d\d/.inspect
    #=> "/\\d\\d:\\d\\d/"
/\d\d:\d\d/.source
    #=> "\\d\\d:\\d\\d"
/\d\d:\d\d/.to_s
    #=> "(?-mix:\\d\\d:\\d\\d)"
```

Strings and regular expressions can be used inter-
changeably through most places in the Core API.

Notice that I used a single quote to keep the backslash
from escaping inside the String object before it gets
passes to Regexp.new. As an example of use, you might
ask a user to describe the native date format to input
as YYYY-MM-DD or MM/DD/YY. You can make a Regexp
object from this as follows:

```
Regexp.new gets.chomp.gsub(%r{[^/]}, '\d')
```

In plain English, this means: "Get a line of input, strip
white space from the ends, replace all occurrences of
characters that are not ^ or / with the String \d (single quoted), and convert the resulting String object
into a Regexp object." Note that %r{} is another way
of writing a regular expression literal—in this case, I
used it to avoid having to escape the /.

Conversely, String representations of the content of a
Regexp can be made.

Note that the last form listed at the beginning of this
subsection is in alternate notation which is more

human-readable; also note that feeding this alternate notation back into Regexp.new might not result in the same Regexp object.

See the subsection "Searching Strings" in "Working with Strings" for more on this topic.

Array to Hash and Back Again

```
Hash[*[1,2,3].zip([4,5,6]).flatten]
    #=> {1=>4, 2=>5, 3=>6}

{ 'foo' => 1, 'bar' => 2, 'baz' => 3 }.keys
    #=> ["baz", "foo", "bar"]

{ 'foo' => 1, 'bar' => 2, 'baz' => 3 }.values
    #=>[3, 1, 2]

{ 'foo' => 1, 'bar' => 2, 'baz' => 3 }.to_a()
    #=> [["baz", 3], ["foo", 1], ["bar", 2]]
```

Above, two ordered Arrays, one with your keys—1, 2, and 3—and another with your values—4, 5, and 6— are zipped together, flattened, and then splatted to make the Array compatible with the Hash.[] class method. This makes the values from the Array become, one, the *key* and, the other, the *value*.

If you have an Array and you want to initialize all of the *keys* of a new Hash but not yet set the *values*, a clever trick is to zip the Array of keys with an empty Array:

```
Hash[*%w{a b c}.zip([]).flatten]
    #=> {"a"=>nil, "b"=>nil, "c"=>nil}
```

Similarly, you can assign the Array's index to the value instead of nil - this requires an interative approach.

```
my_hash = Hash.new
['a','b','c'].each_with_index { |e, i| my_hash[e] =
i }
my_hash
    #=> {"a"=>0, "b"=>1, "c"=>2}[1]
```

You can give the Array class that capability, of course:

```
class Array
    def to_hash
        Hash[*self.zip([]).flatten]
    end
end

[1,2,3].to_hash
    #=> {1=>nil, 2=>nil, 3=>nil}
```

Conversely, you can get the keys and values out of the Hash in a number of ways including those short methods listed at the beginning of this section.

However, you might also want to walk through the Hash and get an Array from keys or values that meet certain criteria:

```
{ 'foo' => 1, 'bar' => 2, 'baz' => 3 }.select do |k,
v|
    v % 2 == 1  # is it odd?
end
    #=> [["baz", 3], ["foo", 1]]
```

See Chapter 3, "Working with Collections," for related topics.

Array **to** Set **and Back Again**

```
require 'set'

['foo', 'bar', 'baz'].to_set
    #=> #<Set: {"baz", "foo", "bar"}>

Set.new(['foo', 'bar', 'baz']).to_a
    #=> ["baz", "foo", "bar"]
```

A Set can be thought of as a Hash with no values (in fact, it uses a Hash for storage). As you can see, converting to a Set from an Array is much easier than from a Hash.

Floating-Point, Integer, and Rational Numbers

```
45 / 5
    #=> 9
45 / 5.0
    #=> 9.0
45.0 / 5
    #=> 9.0
45.0 * 5
    #=> 225.0
45 * 5.0
    #=> 225.0
45 * 5
    #=> 225

Math::PI
    #=> 3.14159265358979
Math::PI.to_i
    #=> 3
Math::PI.ceil
    #=> 4
Math::PI.floor
    #=> 3
Math::PI.round
    #=> 3
```

```
Math::E
    #=> 2.71828182845905
Math::E.round
    #=> 3

7.to_f
    #=> 7.0
```

For the most part, numbers behave in Ruby exactly as they do in other languages. You might be interested in two exceptions, though:

If the `Integer` representation of a number is too large to store in the host machine's CPU registers (larger than 32 bits on x86), the `Integer` representation is stored in a `Bignum` object instead of a `Fixnum` object. The difference between the two is that `Bignum` allows computation on very large (or very negative) numbers at the cost of computational overhead. Note that Ruby uses 1 bit for the sign and 2 more bits for the tag (used for internal bookkeeping).

```
(2**29).class
    #=> Fixnum
(2**30).class
    #=> Bignum
```

Ruby also supports storing numbers in a `Rational` object that implements the normal arithmetic operators.

```
require 'rational'

Rational(3, 4) + Rational(1, 8)
    #=> Rational(7, 8)
Rational(3, 4) / 2
    #=> Rational(3, 8)
```

```
2 * Rational(3, 8)
    #=> Rational(3, 4)
Rational(3, 7).to_f()
    #=> 0.428571428571429
Rational(3, 7).to_s()
    #=> "3/7"
```

A Word on Boolean true and false

In Ruby, anything that is not either false or nil is considered true—even 0 (zero). Let me say that again: 0 evaluates to true. If you want to say that something evaluates to false, you must explicitly state it. If your method needs to return true as the result of some conditional test, just return the test as result as the return value. Remember, the last evaluation in a method is the return value.

As an interesting side note, in Ruby, any time you write out true or false in your code, you are referring to singleton instances of the TrueClass and FalseClass, respectively. So, even true and false have member methods, and variables and respond to method calls.

Working with
Strings

Gluing applications together is what programming languages like Ruby and Perl do particularly well: their text processing facilities are excellent. Whether its parsing configuration files, serving up web pages or capturing the output of a program, you will be working with Strings. Where Ruby and Perl differ, however, is in the object oriented-ness of their approach. In Ruby, Strings have their own member methods which can be accessed to perform each processing function. Keep this in mind throughout this section.

The following subsection and the next two subsections are closely related. I first briefly present the simple searching functions that accept Strings as parameters; then I dive right in to regular expressions.

Searching Strings

```
'foobar'.include? 'fo'
    #=> true
'foobar'['fo']
    #=> "fo "(true because not nil or false)
'foobar'.count 'ob' # 'ob' is taken to be a list of
characters
    #=> 3 (2 "o"s and 1 "b")
'foobar'.count 'ob', 'o'
    #=> 2 (only "o" appeared in both parameters)
'foobar'.index 'ob'
    #=> 2
'foobar'.index 98 # 98 is the ASCII code for 'b'
    #=> 3
```

In the first two examples, #include? is used to find
whether a String includes a substring and return a
Boolean result. This is implemented in C code and is
slightly faster than a Regexp-based search (though, not
by much).

In the middle two examples, #count is used to return
the number of occurrences of a particular string.
Additional parameters to #count are intersected on a
character basis. (*Intersection* is a term from set logic. It
means to only include those elements which occur in
both sets. In this case, an "element" is a character.) This
method is not yet Unicode safe.

Finally, in the last two examples, #index returns the
position—in count-from-zero notation—of the first
occurrence of either a String or the numerical code of
a character. You can use #rindex to find the index of
the last occurrence.

You can also walk through a `String`, `File`, or `IOStream` performing a search. Let's say that you want to write a simple config file parser that places each config variable and its value in a `Hash`:

```
'a = 1\nb = 1\nc = 3\n'.each_line() { |line|
    if line.include?('=')
        # do something with this line
    end
}
```

The code at # is executed only if = is present. See the subsection "Parsing a Simple Config File," in Chapter 7, "Manipulating Text," for a much more complete example of this.

Searching Strings with Regular Expressions

```
"The time is: 12:34:54\n".match
/(\d{2}):(\d{2}):(\d{2})/
    #=> #<MatchData:0x402e9548>
$1
    #=> "12"
$2
    #=> "34"
$3
    #=> "54"
```

This topic is huge—entire books are devoted to regular expressions. Perhaps the best one is *Mastering Regular Expressions* (O'Reilly, 2002), by Jeffrey E. F. Friedl. If your job includes working with a lot of clear text, I highly recommend that you pick up this resource and keep it within reach.

Here I cover ways in which you can use Regexp objects to search text in Ruby (it's not a review of the regular expression language).

When performing a Regexp match in Ruby, any () groupings within the Regexp are set to the (thread-local) global variables $1 to $9 in the order they appear in the Regexp.

The #match method returns a MatchData object *for the first match* in the String and also sets the global variable $~ to the same object. Here's what a MatchData has in it:

```
m = "The time is: 12:34:54\n".match
/(\d{2}):(\d{2}):(\d{2})/
m.to_a
    #=> ["12:34:54", "12", "34", "54"]
m.pre_match
    #=> "The time is: "
m.post_match
    #=> "\n"
```

You can also access the entire match with m[0], and each of the submatches with m[1] to m[9].

If you want to return *all* the matches in the String, use .#scan. This returns an Array that looks like this:

```
"The time is: 12:34:54\n".scan(/\d{2}/)
    #=> ["12", "34", "54"]
```

If you use grouping parentheses in your Regexp, it returns nested Arrays.

You can also use .#split with Strings using regular expressions:

```
"The time is: 12:34:54\n".split(/:\s/)
    #=> ["The time is", "12:34:54\n"]
```

Replacing Substrings

```
s = 'foobar'
s[-1] = 'z'
    s #=> "foobaz"
s[0,4] = 'ja'
    s #=> "jaaz"
s[2] = 122
    s #=> "jazz"

ary = ['some_variable','some_value']

"Setting #{ary[0]} is currently set to #{ary[1]}."
    #=> "Setting some_variable is currently set to
some_value."

"You are currently looking at #{ary[0].tr('_', '
')}."
    #=>"You are currently looking at some variable."
```

As mentioned in the section "String to Array and Back
Again," in Chapter 1, "Converting Between Types,"
Strings can be treated like Arrays of characters in
many respects. This includes replacements such as
above.

In the last two examples above, double-quoted Strings
are used to evaluate "#{}" clauses within them and
interpolate the result of the evaluation. You can do
pretty much anything inside a "#{}". In the above
examples I show array access and even a #tr
method call.

A somewhat more obscure function, #tr allows you to
do a character-wise replacement:

```
'You are currently looking at a string.'.tr 'aeiou',
'_'
    #=> "Y__ _r_ c_rr_ntly l__k_ng _t _ str_ng."
'You are currently looking at a string.'.tr 'aeiou',
'uoiea'
    #=> "Yea uro carrontly leeking ut u string."
```

The first example replaces all vowels with an "_" character; the second switches each vowel for another
vowel. See the subsection "Sanitizing Input," later
in this chapter, for another example of using #tr
and a discussion of how #tr parameters work.

Replacing Substrings using SprintF

```
'I received %25s' % 'a string.'
    #=> "I received                  a string."
'I received %-25s' % 'a string.'
    #=> "I received a string.               "
'I received a couple of strings: %s, %s' % ['one',
'two']
    #=> "I received a couple of strings: one, two"

'I received %25p' % [['an', 'array']]
    #=> "I received           [\"an\", \"array\"]"
'I received %-25p' % [['an', 'array']]
    #=> "I received [\"an\", \"array\"]           "
```

As with numbers, you can also apply sprintf style
formatting using the "%" operator. Table 2.1 gives the
allowed arguments.

Table 2.1   **String SprintF Codes**

String Argument	Arguments Allowed	Explanation
c	*, -	Expects a Fixnum representing character code
s	*, -	Expects a String object
p	*, -	Any object that responds to .inspect()

And Table 2.2 lists what those arguments do.

Table 2.2   **String SprintF Arguments**

Argument	Explanation
*d	d must be an integer. Specifies the width of the field.
-	Left justification.

I should also briefly mention a somewhat obscure feature of sprintf: You can use (position)$ positional notation to access a specific entry in the array provided. Somewhat annoyingly, however, the notation for this access counts starting at 1 instead of 0 (as Arrays do):

```
'Hi %1$s! Today you turn %2$d! Happy birthday,
%1$s!' % ['Joe', 13]
    #=> "Hi Joe! Today you turn 13! Happy birthday,
Joe!"
```

Replacing Substrings using Regular Expressions

```
'The current time is: 12:34:21'.sub(
                     /(\d\d):(\d\d):(\d\d)/,
                     '\1\2\3')
   #=> "The current time is: 123421"
```

Again, you can use regular expressions for some powerful functions. Use \1 to \9 to interpolate the grouping parentheses' results from the match to your replacement. Use .#gsub instead of .#sub to replace all occurrences in a String.

In the example above, the entire phrase "12:34:21" is match and replaced with the subgroups 1-3 with no ":"s between them. Alternatively, you could simply replace any occurrence of ":" appearing between digits.

This could be written like this:

```
'The current time is: 12:34:21'.gsub(
                     /(\d):(\d)/,
                     '\1\2')
   #=> "The current time is: 123421"
```

Working with Unicode

```
#!/usr/bin/ruby -wKu

'цитрус'.scan(/./)  { |b| print b, ' ' }
```

Produces:
ц и т р у с

Ruby accepts source files encoded in UTF-8. Just to be safe, include the -Ku command-line option in your shebang line to ensure that this is properly interpreted on other OSs and other locales. The modified shebang line is the first line in the code sample above.

Ruby itself is not yet fully internationalized. For instance, Ruby is unaware of the multibyte nature of UTF-8 beyond the first 255 character codes. So #each_byte must be used with care when dealing with international strings; for example, it will not work on any non-Latin languages:

```
puts "цитрус" # output directly to buffer
"цитрус".each_byte { |b| print(""<<b, ' ') }
```

Produces:

```
цитрус
? ? ? ? ? ?
```

Instead, use the Regexp engine to iterate over these characters (it is UTF-8 aware). The code to do this is the code sample at the beginning of this section.

In general, use the Regexp engine for slicing and matching when you're working with Unicode. Other than that, Strings with Unicode content should behave exactly as you expect them to.

Sanitizing Input

```
new_password = gets
if new_password.count '^A-Za-z._' != 0 then
    puts "Bad Password"
else
    #do something like in subsection "Encrypting a
String"
end
```

Let's say that you want to write a password changer for *nix (perhaps storing to an LDAP back end). At a login prompt, you can use *almost* all characters in a password that you can generate at a keyboard. But the few that you can't use might give your users a headache when they discover that they can't log in again after changing their password. In an effort to make your life easier, you could write a password changer that restricts the password to alphanumeric and a few of its friends. String#count, as applied above, can help you do just that.

This works by using a special syntax that's shared by .#count, .#tr, #delete, and #squeeze. A parameter beginning with ^ negates the list; the list consists of any valid characters in the active character set and may contain ranges formed with -. If more than one parameter list is given to these functions, the lists of characters are intersected using set logic—that is, only characters in both lists are used for filtering.

For other types of sanitation, you might also want to simply replace all "evil" characters with _ (such as perhaps from a CGI form post):

```
evil_input = '`cat /etc/passwd`'
evil_input.tr('./\`', '_')
    #=> "_cat _etc_passwd_"
```

Working with Line Endings

When dealing with clear text from the three main OS types, you will encounter what is perhaps their oldest file format fragmentation (see Table 2.3).

Table 2.3 **OS-Specific Line Endings**

OS	Line Ending
Mac OS 9 and older	\r
Windows	\r\n
*nix	\n

If you are dealing with Windows and *nix text, you
probably don't need to give it another thought; they
are handled almost exactly the same:

```
"a\r\nb\r\nc\r\n".each_line { |line|
    puts(line.inspect)
}
```

Produces:

```
"a\r\n"
"b\r\n"
"c\r\n"
```

```
"a\r\nb\r\nc\r\n".each_line { |line|
    puts(line.chomp.inspect) # chomp safely removes
both
}
```

Produces:

```
"a"
"b"
"c"
```

On Linux it looks almost identical:

```
"a\nb\nc\n".each_line { |line|
    puts(line.inspect)
}
```

Produces:

```
"a\n"
"b\n"
"c\n"
```

For Mac OS files, you need to specify the separator:

```
"a\rb\rc\r".each_line "\r" { |line|
    puts(line.inspect)
}
```

Produces:

```
"a\r"
"b\r"
"c\r"
```

Processing Large Strings

```
my_string = ''
(2**21).times{ my_string << rand(256) }
    #=> 2097152 (2 MB of random data)

require 'stringio'
string_stream = StringIO.new my_string
string_stream.read 256
    #=> "\351@\300g\251\326\036\314| *\335jJ\017 ...
```

When such a huge String is already in memory, the best way to handle it depends on what you are going to do with it. If the String is clear text and you intend to parse it somehow, make use of #each_line. Refer to the subsection "Building a Hash from a Config File," in Chapter 3, for an example of building a Hash from such a String. However, if the String contains binary data, you can take slices of predetermined amounts of bytes at a time, such has been shown above in increments of 256. In this example, every time #read is called, an Enumerator (a kind of position marker) moves to keep track of your position in the String.

Comparing Strings

```
"Who" <=> "who"
    #=> -1
%w{'who' 'is' 'on' 'first?' 'Who'}.sort
    #=> ["Who", "first?", "is", "on", "who"]
'foobar'.casecmp 'Foobaz'
    #=> -1
'foobar'.casecmp 'FooBar'
    #=> 0
%w{'who' 'is' 'on' 'first?' 'Who'}.sort { |a,b|
a.casecmp b }
    #=> ["first?", "is", "on", "who", "Who"]
```

You can compare Strings in a case-sensitive manner— this is how #sort works by default. Non-case-sensitive comparisons are now handled by String#casecmp. This method works in the same way that "<=>" does (returning -1, 0, or 1), so it can be used as a part of "#sort {}" calls.

Checksumming a String (MD5 or Otherwise)

```
require 'digest/md5'
Digest::MD5::new 'foobar'
    #=> 3858f62230ac3c915f300c664312c63f
require 'digest/sha1'
Digest::SHA1::new 'foobar'
    #=> 8843d7f92416211de9ebb963ff4ce28125932878
```

Above, I show both MD5 and SHA1 checksum methods. Be aware that MD5 has been shown to be weak—with some effort, someone could generate a file which has the same MD5 sum thereby impersonating a valid file. You can use SHA1 instead as I have show above.

If you need to checksum a file, one approach is to #read the whole file in to a String and perform the previous methods. However, this is a bad idea if you are checksumming any kind of large file. Instead, consider the following approach:

```ruby
require 'digest/md5'

def md5sum_file path
  d = Digest::MD5.new
  File.open(path, 'r') do |fp|
    while buf = fp.read(1024*8)
      d << buf
    end
  end
  d.hexdigest
```

The above example uses the #update or #<< method of MD5, and doesn't require the whole file to be read into memory.

Encrypting a String

```ruby
password = 'f00bar'

# generate a random salt
salting_chars = ('A'..'Z').to_a + ('a'..'z').to_a +
['.', '/']
salt = salting_chars[rand(54)] +
salting_chars[rand(54)]
    #=> "jM"
```

```
password.crypt(salt)
    #=> "jM7qRC1u1BPhc"
```

String#crypt enables you to perform a one-way hash
function on a String. This can be used for simple password security. To store the password for the first time,
choose a random salt and then use that to hash the
password that you received. Notice that the salt is
stored at the beginning of the hash (which is the last
line in the above example). You can use that hash to
verify someone trying to use this password. Because
this is a one-way encryption, you must encrypt the
attempted password with the same salt and compare
the two encrypted strings to find out whether they
are equal:

```
input_password = 'f00bar'
crypted_password = 'jM7qRC1u1BPhc'

salt =  crypted_password[0,2]
    #=> "jM"

# test password
input_password.crypt(salt) ==  crypted_password
```

If you would like to implement a two-way encryption
(one that requires that some kind of key be provided
to decrypt the text), there is no such class or method
in the standard Ruby library. Consider using the
Ruby-AES module from RAA. On some operating
systems, the output of a subprocess "aesloop" command could also be used.

Working with Collections

In Ruby and other dynamic languages, "Collection" is an umbrella term for general-use lists and hashes. The ease of working with these data structures is an attractive feature and one that often contributes to making prototyping in Ruby a pleasurable experience. The implementation details of lists and hashes and their underlying mechanisms are mostly hidden from the programmer leaving him to focus on his work.

As you browse this section, keep in mind that underpinning everything you see here are traditional C-based implementations of lists and hashes; Ruby is attempting to save you the trouble of working with C—but be sure, that trouble saving can come at performance cost.

Slicing an Array

This section has a lot of analogs to the earlier section "String to Array and Back Again," in Chapter 1, "Converting Between Types." You can slice an Array a number of ways:

```
[1, 2, 3, 4, 5, 6, 7, 8, 9][4]
   #=> 5 (a Fixnum object)

[1, 2, 3, 4, 5, 6, 7, 8, 9][4,1]
   #=> [5] (single element Array)

[1, 2, 3, 4, 5, 6, 7, 8, 9][4,2]
   #=> [5, 6]

[1, 2, 3, 4, 5, 6, 7, 8, 9][-4,4]
   #=> [6, 7, 8, 9]

[1, 2, 3, 4, 5, 6, 7, 8, 9][2..5]
   #=> [3, 4, 5, 6]

[1, 2, 3, 4, 5, 6, 7, 8, 9][-4..-1]
   #=> [6, 7, 8, 9]

[1, 2, 3, 4, 5, 6, 7, 8, 9][2...5]
   #=> [3, 4, 5]

[1, 2, 3, 4, 5, 6, 7, 8, 9][-4...-1]
   #=> [6, 7, 8]

[1, 2, 3, 4, 5, 6, 7, 8, 9][4..200]
   #=> [5, 6, 7, 8, 9] (no out of range error!)
```

Array Ranges	Positions (Counting Starts at 0, Negative Numbers Count Position from the End)
A[{start}..{end}]	{start} includes the element; {end} includes the element
A[{start}...{end}]	{start} includes the element; {end} excludes the element
A[{start}, {count}]	{start} includes the element; {count} positions from start to include

You might also like to select elements from the Array if certain criteria are met:

```
[1, 2, 3, 4, 5, 6, 7, 8, 9].select { |element| ele-
ment % 2 == 0 }
    #=> [2, 4, 6, 8] (all the even elements)
```

Iterating over an Array

```
[1, 2, 3, 4, 5].each do |element|
    # do something to element
end
```

This is one of the joys of Ruby. It's so easy!

You can also do the trusty old for loop:

```
for element in [1, 2, 3, 4, 5]
    # do something to element
end
```

The difference between a for loop and an #each is that in for, a new lexical scoping is not created. That is, any variables that are created by for or that are in the loop remain after the loop ends.

To traverse the Array in reverse, you can simply use #Array#reverse#each. Note that in this case, a copy of the Array is being made by #reverse, and then #each is called on that copy. If your Array is very large, this could be a problem.

In order for you get any more specialized than that, however, you need to work with the Enumerator module. For example, you might want to traverse an Array processing five elements at a time as opposed to the one element yielded by #each:

```
require 'enumerator'
ary = [0, 1, 2, 3, 4, 5, 6, 7, 8, 9]
ary.each_slice(5) { |element| p element }
```

Outputs:

```
[0, 1, 2, 3, 4]
[5, 6, 7, 8, 9]
```

Creating Enumerable Classes

You may find that you need to make information in a
given, custom data structure available to the rest of the
world. In such a case, if the data structure that you
have created to store arbitrary objects implements an
#each method, the Enumerable mix-in will allow any-
one who uses your class to access several traversal and
searching methods, for free.

```
require 'enumerator'

class NumberStore
      include Enumerable

      attr_reader :neg_nums, :pos_nums

      def add foo_object
            if foo_object.respond_to? :to_i
                  foo_i = foo_object.to_i
                  if foo_i < 0
                        @neg_nums.push foo_i
                  else
                        @pos_nums.push foo_i
                  end
            else
```

```
                            raise "Not a number."
                end
        end

        def each
                @neg_nums.each { |i| yield i }
                @pos_nums.each { |i| yield i }
        end

        def initialize
                @neg_nums = []
                @pos_nums = []
        end
end

mystore = NumberStore.new
mystore.add 5
mystore.add 87
mystore.add(-92)
mystore.add(-1)

p mystore.neg_nums
p mystore.pos_nums

p mystore.grep -50..60
```

Produces:

```
[-92, -1]
[5, 87]
[-1, 5]
```

In the above contrived example, I have created a data structure called NumberStore which stores negative numbers in one list and positive numbers in another list. Because the #each method is implemented, methods like #find, #select, #map, and #grep become available. In the last line of the code sample I use the mixed-in method #grep to find numbers stored in mystore that are between 50 and 60.

Sorting an Array

```
[5, 2, 1, 4, 3].sort
   #=> [1, 2, 3, 4, 5]
```

As long as all the objects stored in the Array respond to the <=> method, the Array will be sorted successfully. If you want to sort by some special criteria, you can supply a block or even map a value to each element that *can* be compared using "<=>". Here is a somewhat contrived example (there are many ways to accomplish this):

```
['Platinum', 'Gold', 'Silver', 'Copper'].sort_by do
|award|
    case award
    when 'Platinum': 4
    when 'Gold': 3
    when 'Silver': 2
    when 'Copper': 1
    else 0
    end
end
    #=> ["Copper", "Silver", "Gold", "Platinum"]
```

Above, a numerical value is assigned to each String and then the Array is sorted by #sort_by using those values.

Word of warning: When sorting numerical values, beware of Floats, they can have the value NaN (imaginary) which is, of course, not comparable to real numbers. Array#sort will fail if your array has such a NaN:

```
[1/0.0, 1, 0, -1, -1/0.0, (-1)**(0.5)]
    #=> [Infinity, 1, 0, -1, -Infinity, NaN]
[1/0.0, 1, 0, -1, -1/0.0, (-1)**(0.5)].sort
```

Produces:

```
ArgumentError: comparison of Fixnum with Float
failed
```

Iterating over Nested Arrays

Array.flatten.each { |elem| #do something }

You can #flatten the Array as I have done above. For
most cases, this works just fine—it's very fast. But it's
perhaps not quite as flexible as a recursive implementation:

```
class Array
    def each_recur(&block)
        each do |elem|
            if elem.is_a? Array
                elem.each_recur &block
            else
                block.call elem
            end
        end
    end
end

my_ary = [[1, 2, 3, 4],[5, 6, 7, 8]]
    #=> [[1, 2, 3, 4], [5, 6, 7, 8]]

my_ary.each_recur { |elem| print(elem, " ") }
```

Produces:

```
1 2 3 4 5 6 7 8
```

Modifying All the Values in an Array

Array#collect, also known as Array#map, is used to modify the values of an Array and return a new array.

```
['This', 'is', 'a', 'test!'].collect do |word|
    word.downcase.delete '^A-Za-z'
end
    #=> ["this", "is", "a", "test"]
```

If you want to do this on a nested Array, you need something a little stronger:

```
class Array
    def collect_recur(&block)
        collect do |e|
            if e.is_a? Array
                e.collect_recur(&block)
            else
                block.call(e)
            end
        end
    end
end

[[1,2,3],[4,5,6]].collect_recur { |elem| elem**2 }
    #=> [[1, 4, 9], [16, 25, 36]]
```

Sorting Nested Arrays

```
[[36, 25, 16], [9, 4, 1]].flatten.sort
    #=> [1, 4, 9, 16, 25, 36]
```

We have to #flatten the Array because the #sort uses <=> to compare two Arrays, which in turn, compares their elements for either all elements being less than all elements in the other Array or vice-versa (if neither condition is met they are considered equal). It doesn't descend in to the Arrays to sort them. Here is what would happen if we didn't flatten:

```
[[36, 25, 16], [9, 4, 1]].sort
    #=> [[9, 4, 1], [36, 25, 16]]
```

Once again, the first code will work in most cases but a recursive implementation is able to accommodate working with the Array in place without destroying the heirarchy (note that this sorts in place, for simplicity):

```
class Array
    def sort_recur!
        sort! do |a,b|
            a.sort_recur! if a.is_a? Array
            b.sort_recur! if b.is_a? Array
            a <=> b
        end
    end
end

p [[36, 25, 16], [9, 4, 1]].sort_recur!
```

Produces:

```
[[1, 4, 9], [16, 25, 36]]
```

Building a Hash from a Config File

```
my_hash = Hash::new
tmp_ary = Array::new

"a = 1\nb = 2\nc = 3\n".each_line do |line|
    if line.include? '='
        tmp_ary = line.split('=').collect { |s|
s.strip }
        my_hash.store(*tmp_ary)
    end
end

p tmp_ary
p my_hash
Produces:
["c", "3"] (from the last loop)
{"a"=>"1", "c"=>"3", "b"=>"2"}
```

This is very similar to an earlier example in the section "Searching Strings," in Chapter 2, "Working With Strings." Here we are processing a simple format config file. This is a sample of what such a file looks like:

```
variable1 = foo
variable2 = bar
variable3 = baz
```

For the sake of simplicity, instead of a File for simulated input, this example uses a simple String with some \n (newline) separators.

In plain English, those inner lines mean, "Take the current line and call the #split on it, splitting on the '=' character; pass each element of the resulting two-element Array in to the block; call the #strip method on the Strings to remove any whitespace, and return the modified Array to tmp_ary. Hash#store expects two parameters, not an Array, so we use the splat (*) operator to expand the tmp_ary Array down so that it appears to be a list of parameters."

Sorting a Hash by Key or Value

```
my_hash = {'a'=>'1', 'c'=>'3', 'b'=>'2'}
my_hash.keys.sort.each { |key| puts my_hash[key] }
Produces:
1
2
3
```

Hashes are unsorted objects because of the way in which they are stored internally. If you want to access a Hash in a sorted manner by *key*, you need to use an Array as an indexing mechanism as is shown above.

You can also use the Hash#sort method to get a new sorted Array of pairs:

```
my_hash.sort
    #=> [["a", "1"], ["b", "2"], ["c", "3"]]
```

You can do the same by *value*, but it's a little more complicated:

```
my_hash.keys.sort_by { |key| my_hash[key] }.each do
|key|
    puts my_hash[key]
end
```

Or, you can use the Hash#sort method for values:

```
my_hash.sort { |l, r| l[1]<=>r[1] }
    #=> [["a", "1"], ["b", "2"], ["c", "3"]]
```

This works by using the Emmuerator#sort_by method
that is mixed into the Array of keys. #sort_by looks at
the value my_hash[key] returns to determine the sorting order.

Eliminating Duplicate Data from Arrays (Sets)

```
[1, 1, 2, 3, 4, 4].uniq
    #=> [1, 2, 3, 4]
```

You can approach this problem in two different ways.
If you are adding all your data to your Array up front,
you can use the expensive way, #uniq, above, because
you have to do it only once.

But if you will constantly be adding and removing data
to your collection and you need to know that all the
data is unique at any time, you need something more
to guarantee that all your data is unique, but without a
lot of cost. A set does just that.

Sets are a wonderful tool: They ensure that the values
you have stored are unique. This is accomplished by
using a Hash for its storage mechanism, which, in turn,
generates a unique signifier for any keys it's storing.
This guarantees that you won't have the same data in
the set while also keeping things accessible and fast!
Beware, however, sets are not ordered.

```
require 'set'
myset = Set::new [1, 1, 2, 3, 4, 4]
    #=> #<Set: {1, 2, 3, 4}>
```

Adding duplicate data causes no change:

```
myset.add 4
    #=> #<Set: {1, 2, 3, 4}>
```

Working with Nested Sets

You should be aware that Set does not guarantee that nested sets stored in it are unique. This is because foo_set.eql? bar_set will never return true - even if the sets have exactly the same values in them. Other kinds of objects in Ruby exhibit this behavior, so keep your eyes open.

If you would like to iterate over the contents of sets without having to worry about the nested data possibly colliding with the upper data, you cannot use Set#flatten. Here is a simple method to recursively walk through such a set:

```
class Set
    def each_recur(&block)
        each do |elem|
            if elem.is_a? Set
                elem.each_recur(&block)
            else
                block.call(elem)
            end
        end
    end
end

my_set = Set.new.add([1, 2, 3, 4].to_set).add([1, 2,
3, 4].to_set)
    #=> #<Set: {#<Set: {1, 2, 3, 4}>, #<Set: {1, 2,
```

```
3, 4}>}>

my_set.each_recur { |elem| print(elem, " ") }
```

Produces:

```
1 2 3 4 1 2 3 4
```

4

Working with Objects

Working in Ruby is a joy because there is an internal consistency to the design. This consistency leads to expected ("least surprising") behavior throughout the core Ruby classes, and this section is about that design. First, some ground rules:

An important detail to remember when working with Ruby is that all objects are subclassed from Object in some way; indeed, every object class that you create yourself will be a subclass of the class Class; in turn, Class is a subclass of Object. As I mention later, every new class also mixes in methods and properties of the Module class.

Object also mixes in methods from the Kernel module. This ensures that methods such as #gets, #puts, and #p work no matter which scope you call them in. So to recap, every single class or instance of that class will have methods and properties that come from all four of these classes:

- Object
- Kernel

- Class
- Module

You would be well on your way to zen mastery of Ruby if you were intimately familiar with the documentation for those four classes. But for now, let's look at some specifics.

Inspecting Objects and Classes

```
# Class inspections
String.methods
String.constants

# Instance inspections
my_string = String.new
my_string.instance_methods
my_string.constants
my_string.instance_variables
my_string.object_id
```

One of the really great tools in the Ruby toolbox is irb. At the irb console (and inside your program), you can inspect just about everything: modules, classes, and objects. You can examine internal states of variables and constants, internal methods, access restrictions, and even information about each existence inside the Ruby VM. I have provided some examples of these capabilities.

String Presentation of Objects

```
h = { "a" => 123, "b" => 456, "c" => 789 }
p h
f = File.open "Ruby Book/test.txt"
p f
```

This code produces the following output:

```
{"a"=>123, "b"=>456, "c"=>789}
#<File:Ruby Book/test.txt>
```

The #inspect method, as a Ruby convention, is expected to return a human-readable String representing the object. The Ruby method #p expects all objects to respond to this method call.

#inspect is also the method that irb uses to display the results of evaluating a line. Consider implementing #inspect in any classes that you will create. Doing so enables you to more easily inspect your classes from within irb, which anyone using your code will certainly appreciate.

Ruby-Style Polymorphisms ("Duck Typing")

```
def second_item(obj)
  return obj[1] if obj.respond_to? :[]
end
```

The Pragmatic Programmers have introduced the Ruby community to a style of programming called duck typing. In this way of looking at an object's type, to borrow from a colloquialism—"If it looks like a duck and walks like a duck, it is a duck." So rather than ask, "Is this object an instance of Foo class?" we ask, "Does this object respond to #foo method?"

For example, let's say that I want to write a method called #second_item. This method would be designed with things like Arrays in mind: simply retrieving position [1] from the Array and returning it. It could be written this way:

```
def second(obj)
  return obj[1] if obj.kind_of? Array
end
```

But if I apply the principle of duck typing—illustrated in the code snippet earlier in this section—I can get support for any class that implements the #[] method. So now, using the snippet of code from earlier, I can even #second_item a String:

```
mystring = 'Hello World!'

second_item mystring
  #=> 101 # the ASCII code for 'e'
```

But this philosophy has its problems, too. For instance, is #second_item meaningful when called on a Hash? Hash certainly responds to the #[] method call, but because instances of Hash are not ordered, looking up a hash key named "[1]" does not have any ordered significance.

Comparing Objects

```
a = 42
b = 42
a == b
                                       #=> true
a.object_id == b.object_id            #=> false

a = 42
b = a
a == b
                                       #=> true
a.object_id == b.object_id
          #=> true
```

It is important to differentiate between two different types of specific equality in Ruby: that which is of *equal value* and that which has an *equal identity*.

For instance, two objects have equal value if their *stored values* are equal. In the first case provided, the `Fixnum` class implements a `#==` method, which compares the `values` of `self` (the stored numerical value). However, we can also talk about whether two objects are actually the same object inside the Ruby VM. For example, in the second case provided, their object IDs are equal.

A quick side note: The `#===` method (not to be confused with `#==`) is generally used by classes to tell you whether two objects are instances of the same class. However, many classes override this method to provide special meaning for `#===`. For comparing `class` membership, use the `#kind_of?` method.

Serializing Objects

```
h = { "a" => 123 }

Marshal.dump h

            #=> "\004\b{\006\"\006ai\001{"
Marshal.load "\004\b{\006\"\006ai\001{"      #=>
{"a"=>123}
```

This example code converts a Ruby object in to a String representation of its internal state. The same String representation can be parsed by `Marshal#load` to obtain the original object.

Objects can be converted to `Strings` for long-term storage. Between minor releases of Ruby, the storage format does not change. You can use this mechanism to store the state of your Ruby programs to files, or even to send them over IO streams to other Ruby programs of the same major version. DRB, included in the Standard Library, uses this feature to allow inter-Ruby script communication over sockets.

Duplication

```
a = Hash.new
b = a.dup
a.object_id
  #=> -605558818
b.object_id
  #=> -605579038
```

You can use #dup and #clone to duplicate objects. The difference between the two is this: #clone copies the state of the object in the VM to a new memory location; #dup generally attempts to use the class's own #initialize method.

Notice that the internal state of the object can refer to other objects in the VM. If so, those references still refer to the same objects—even though they were copied. For instance, consider a Hash of Hashes:

```
a = 'foo'
b = { 'bar' => 'baz' }
  #=> {"bar"=>"baz"}
c = {a, b }
  #=> {"foo"=>{"bar"=>"baz"}}

d = c.dup
  #=> {"foo"=>{"bar"=>"baz"}}

# it didn't duplicate the nested Hash
d[a].object_id
=> -739733318
b.object_id
=> -739733318
```

This happens because we are not making a deep copy.
To implement a deep copy, you can use the "Marshal
copy trick":

```ruby
a = 'foo'
b = { 'bar' => 'baz' }
  #=> {"bar"=>"baz"}
c = {a, b }
  #=> {"foo"=>{"bar"=>"baz"}}

d = Marshal.load(Marshal.dump(c))
  #=> {"foo"=>{"bar"=>"baz"}}

# this time they nested Hashes are in separate
memory
d[a].object_id
  #=> -739819088
b.object_id
  #=> -739733318
```

See the chapter "Working with Collections" for examples of recursive algorithms which can be used to perform deep copies.

Protecting an Object Instance

```ruby
a = Hash.new
a.freeze
a['Foo'] = 'Bar' # error
```

You can freeze an object, to prevent it from being
manipulated, by using the #freeze instance method.
This is useful when you want to encourage clients of
your class to #dup or #clone your object before working with it.

This code produces the following output:

```
TypeError: can't modify frozen hash
```

Note, however, that frozen objects *can* be reclaimed by the garbage collector (such as when they fall out of scope).

Garbage Collecting

```
GC.start
```

Using the previous code causes the garbage collector to be invoked manually. You might use this code when you've just finished processing a very large data set and you know that now would be a good time to flush all information that has fallen out of scope.

Note that Ruby will block (pause execution of scripts) while the garbage collector is being run. To prevent this from accidentally happening in the middle of some critical stream-processing code, you can turn off the GC temporarily:

```
GC.disable
```

The garbage-collection system in Ruby is mostly out-of-sight, out-of-mind. And really, that's a good thing. It does a pretty good job and generally stays out of your way. But it might be interesting to know what's going on behind-the-scenes. Let's take a look at the ObjectSpace module.

You can use ObjectSpace to iterate over every item currently in the Ruby VM:

```
ObjectSpace.each_object {|x| p x }
```

However, you might want to limit it to only objects that are instances of a certain class or module:

```
# show all open files
ObjectSpace.each_object(File) {|x| p x }
```

You might also want to know *when* an object is being garbage-collected. ObjectSpace provides a handy way of attaching a method that will be executed when an object is deleted:

```
begin
    a = {}
    ObjectSpace.define_finalizer( a,
        proc {puts "Deleted Hash"} )
end
```

This code produces the following output when the object is GC'd:

```
Deleted Hash
```

Using Symbols

```
method(:foobar).call()
```

What does this statement mean? Read literally, one could say, "Look up the method foobar() and call it." Except for the overhead of calling two additional methods, this is exactly equivalent to this:

```
foobar()
```

Of all the topics in Ruby, the topic of Symbols is perhaps the most difficult to grasp. (To the programmer who is coming from Lisp or Smalltalk, you can think of Symbols as "symbols" or "atoms," respectively.) The most important thing to remember is that a Symbol is a unique name, contains only its own name, and always contains its own name.

It's popular to respond to queries about symbols by saying "Symbols are just immutable strings." But this analogy really doesn't hold. Perhaps the best way to explain a Symbol is to cut around the analogies and go straight to the technical issue.

As you already know, function names in Ruby must be unique in the context in which they are called; otherwise, how will Ruby know which method to call? So why not simply call a method by a String that the programmer can personally verify is unique? Well, Ruby enables you to do that if you want:

```
method('foobar').call()
```

Notice that this is very similar to the first code snippet in this subsection. This is primarily because it has become a convention to automatically convert String parameters to Symbols inside methods that expect Symbols.

This need for uniqueness is the real reason Symbols are used in Ruby (or any other language) and is motivated by the way programming languages store information about the local context. When you call the method foo(), Ruby checks a hash table of all the methods that you (and Ruby) have defined. Because no two hashes of any word are ever equal, this ensures that each unique method name has a unique position in this hash table. Almost all programming languages use a hash to optimize lookup of methods and variables. In Ruby's case, a Symbol is a precomputed hash. That is, a Symbol is computed into its equivalent hash value at parse time. If you were to use Strings to refer to internal objects, Ruby would have to compute the hash value of that String every time it encountered it during the execution of your program.

Anywhere the literal :my_symbol appears in your code, it refers *immediately* to the point in the hash table where any variable or method named my_symbol *must* be stored. This brings up another point: In the same

way that 1 == 1 and 256 == 256, the symbol :foo ==
:foo. :foo always computes to the same hash value;
therefore, it has exactly the same value everywhere.

This property can be used throughout Ruby to speed
things up a bit. This benchmark demonstrates the overhead of having to compute the String hash each time
that a method expecting a Symbol receives one.

```ruby
require 'benchmark'

def foobar
  # pass
end

n = 500000

Benchmark.bmbm do |bench|
  bench.report('Symbol') do
    n.times { method(:foobar).call() }
  end
  bench.report('String') do
    n.times { method('foobar').call() }
  end
end
```

This code produces the following output:

```
Rehearsal --------------------
Symbol 1.020000 0.090000 1.110000 ( 1.134434)
String 1.280000 0.080000 1.360000 ( 1.392788)
---------------- total: 2.470000sec

        user    system   total    real
Symbol 1.040000 0.070000 1.110000 ( 1.133537)
String 1.270000 0.100000 1.370000 ( 1.401934)
```

Remember, it's convention to allow programmers to
also use a String anywhere they use a Symbol, so be

sure to take this into account when writing your own
methods. As an example, this is a (simple) version of
the built-in attr_reader() function. It accepts a Symbol
just like the built-in method.

```
class Module

  # Classes mix-in the Module class, so adding
  # it here
makes it available everywhere. We take
  # the Symbol or
String provided and add a @ to the
  # front to allow us
reference the instance
  # variable.

  def my_attr_reader sym
    define_method(sym) do
      instance_variable_get('@' + sym.to_s)
    end
  end
end

class Foobar
  def initialize n
    @inst_var = n
  end

  my_attr_reader :inst_var

end

a = Foobar.new 'baz'
puts a.inst_var
```

This code produces the following output:

```
baz
```

5

Working with Pipes

A quick review for those who don't swim in *nix operating systems or aren't familiar with pipes from other programming experience:

Every program has three basic file descriptors: 0, 1, and 2. These file descriptors have been traditionally named STDIN, STDOUT, and STDERR, respectively—commonly referred to as *pipes*. Most programs output any kind of error message to STDERR. In addition, any sort of output that you might want to display, pipe to a file, or parse is output to STDOUT. STDIN is used for either interactive keyboard input or to receive input from another program's STDOUT. Here is an example of such a link between programs using pipes; the link is created by the use of the pipe (|) character in the shell:

```
ruby -e 'puts "Hello World!"' | awk '{print $1}'
```

This produces the following output:

```
Hello
```

In this example, Ruby outputs its command-line parameter to its STDOUT. The shell has linked the STDOUT of Ruby to the STDIN of **awk. awk** has been instructed to print the first column of every line that it receives on STDIN. **awk's** output is not being directed to another program, so it is output to the screen.

In Ruby, when we use Kernel#puts or *Kernel#print,* we are sending output to STDOUT by default. If we want to output to STDERR, all we need to do is use STDERR.puts or STDERR.print. For example:

```
DEBUG = true
# ...
STDERR.puts 'An event of some kind has occurred.' if
DEBUG
```

Determining Interactive Standard Pipes

```
if STDIN.tty?
  puts 'Press RETURN to continue.'
  STDIN.readline
end
```

It is important to know whether or not your program's input and output are interactive terminals. For instance, if your program is designed to output progress updates as it continues and STDOUT is interactive, you may wish to output aesthetically pleasing periodic updates of a given task's completeness. Commonly, programs will give their output in the form of a percentage followed by "/r" to return the cursor to the beginning of the same line – repeatedly doing this allows the program to continually provide updates without causing the screen to scroll.

Conversely, you may need to know whether or not
your program is receiving input on STDIN from a
user or from another program. For example, you may
wish to display a prompt if STDIN is interactive and
suppress the prompt if STDIN is a pipe from another
program.

In both cases, the above code can be used to determine whether or not the particular file handle is interactive. However, there are some cases which are troublesome, such as programs started from a crontab. To
ensure absolute correctness, if you want to accept the
standard pipes explicitly, then consider implementing
the Unix convention: a "-" option to indicate a pipe in
place of what otherwise might have been a file argument.

```
if ARGV.delete '-'
  # accept STDIN
end
```

Synchronizing STDERR with STDOUT

```
$stdout.sync = true
$stdin.sync = true
```

One of the many issues you will encounter while
working with Ruby as a system administrator is
obtaining meaningful debugging output. This can be
tricky if your program is also outputting information
to standard out. The reason this is tricky is, to increase
performance, output to both of these file descriptors is
performed *asynchronously*. That is, a buffer is used to
allow program execution to continue while output is
waiting to be placed on the screen.

To make STDOUT and STDERR sync up, we need to write to them *synchronously*. This is done by using the code snippet at the beginning of this subsection. The performance is much lower, but it gives us the meaningful output we want.

As a high-performance alternative, if you don't care whether both your output and your error messages appear on the same pipe, you could use a clever override to catch any calls to $stderr and redirect them to STDOUT.

```
$stderr.reopen $stdout
```

Note that this is not equivalent to using shell redirection. By the time output reaches the shell, it has already passed through a buffer.

Capturing the Output of a Child Process

```
input = IO.popen 'echo hello', 'r'
input.gets
        #=> "hello"
```

The above code simply opens a child process and captures its STDOUT. When we call IO#gets, the last line of output is returned. Beware that buffering can be at play here too. For instance, you may find that you need to call either IO#close_write or IO#close_read in order to cause the respective buffers to be flushed. Otherwise, your program may block waiting for input, forever.

Implementing a Progress Bar

```ruby
# A simulated file copy thread with periodic updates
file_copy = Thread.new do
  Thread.current['progress'] = 0.0
  100.times do
    Thread.current['progress'] += 0.01;
    sleep 0.2
  end
end

until (percent = file_copy['progress']) >= 1.0
  Kernel.sleep 0.1
  print '['
  print '#' * ( 10 * percent ).floor
  print '=' * ( 10 * ( 1.0 - percent) ).ceil
  print "] %-5.1f%%\r" % [percent * 100]
end
puts
```

The STDOUT or STDERR of a subprocess (such as a copy or dd command) can output information about its progress. In the above example, I simulate capturing such output and storing it in a thread shared variable called progress. I use that status and implement a wrapper that displays a progress bar.

Drawing the progress bar is just a matter of doing a little math and using the * operator to multiply the # and = characters. It should look something like this:

[##========] 26.0 %

On your system, you may find that the progress bar does not immediately render each update. To fix that use:

STDOUT.sync

This is so that the progress bar is immediately rendered at each update. to the screen—otherwise, our program will appear stuck.

Creating a Secured Password Prompt

```
system 'stty -echo'
#...
system 'stty echo'
```

The stty magic that was used in the earlier example has the same effect when we're trying to write a secured password prompt. Here I take the example from Chapter 2 "Working with Strings" and implement a password changer:

```
begin

  system 'stty -echo'

  print "New password: "
  p1 = gets
  print "\nReenter password: "
  p2 = gets
  puts
  if p1 == p2 :
    # generate a random salt
    salting_chars = ('A'..'Z').to_a +
('a'..'z').to_a + ['.', '/']
    salt = salting_chars[rand(54)] +
salting_chars[rand(54)]
    p1.crypt salt
    # do something with your new password
  else
    puts 'Passwords do not match.'
  end

# make sure the terminal reenters a usable state
ensure
  system 'stty echo'
end
```

This works because terminals are attached to virtual TTYs, which implement interpretation of ioctl codes. The stty command activates those modes.

It's actually possible to manipulate ioctl directly from inside Ruby for very specialized cases. However, it's somewhat complicated, uglier than even C code, and also very platform specific. If you are interested in exploring this, take a look at your ioctls.h and terminos.h from your OS programming manual. Then the problem looks something like this:

```
orig_devmask = "\0" * 256

# read terminal mask
STDIN.ioctl 0x00005405, orig_devmask

devmask = orig_devmask.unpack 'C4 S'
devmask[4] &= ~0x00000008 # disable echo
devmask = devmask.pack 'C4 S'

# write terminal mask
STDIN.ioctl 0x00005407, devmask

# capture the password here

# restore original mask
STDIN.ioctl 0x00005407, orig_devmask
```

Yeah, ugly.

## 6

Working with Files

In many ways, this chapter is closely related to the previous chapter, "Working with Pipes". The principals are the same because both are implemented as children of the IO class.

Indeed, in Unix, the distinction between IO devices and "files" is significantly blurred. For instance, /dev/random is a "file" in the sense that it has a name and path. But it's also a direct way to "read" the random numbers generator in to any program that accepts files as input.

In Ruby, all IO objects have basic input and output support, depending on which file mode the object was opened with.

Opening and Closing Files

Certainly, one of the tried-and-true conventions in Ruby is using code blocks to ensure that resources are automatically closed.

```
File.open('foobar', 'w') do |file|
 file.puts 'Hello World'
end
```

In the block form—even if there's an event that causes immediate exiting of the program—the file will always be closed properly. This is true when you are doing any form of reading or writing.

You can close a file at any time with File#close. If you are going to close the file conditionally, you might want to insert File#closed? checks throughout your code to avoid running into an IOError exception.

```
begin
  f = File.open "foobar", "w+"
  if true :
    f.close
  end

  # ... some time later ...

  unless f.closed?
    f.rewind
    puts f.gets
    # ...
  end
ensure
  f.close unless f.closed?
end
```

Searching and Seeking Large File Contents

```
File.open 'public_html/index.html', 'r' do |file|
  file.each do |line|
    p $~ if line.match /Jason/i
  end
end
```

The above code is a quick and effective way to search a file. When you are dealing with large files, we want to avoid loading a single large, multiline `String` in to memory. Using the `IO#gets` methods that you are already familiar with, you can open and read file contents one line at a time, searching the contents as you go, such as the method shown above.

However, you can also give `#each` a parameter that indicates the record separator. For instance, you could split on `\n\n`, which would yield *paragraphs* instead of *lines*.

You could also walk though a file a byte at a time. This is handy in files that have no line feeds or concept of a "record separator." I often run into these kinds of files when working with XML (such as that used in SVG); if you don't particularly want to load up a full XML parser, you can instead get some context for the occurrence of your search term.

In this code sample below, I walk through the file 1KB at a time, displaying 80 characters of context for any match.

It works like this: For each chunk read in, I check whether the search `String` is present. If it is, I calculate the position of the match relative to the entire file and then seek to 40 characters earlier in the file and read forward 80 characters (plus some more for the size of the search `String`). I then `#puts` the data read in and set the file position to the character immediately following the match.

If I don't find the search parameter in the chunk, I skip forward 1KB, but I'm sure to decrease that by the size of the search parameter. This is to avoid missing any occurrences that fall on the edge of a 1KB boundary.

```
search = "foo"
File.open('rubbish.svg', 'r') do |file|
  while chunk = file.read 1024      if pos =
chunk.index(search)
      pos = file.pos - (1024 - pos)
      file.seek((pos - 40), IO::SEEK_SET)
      puts file.read(80 + search.size)
      file.seek((pos + search.size), IO::SEEK_SET)
    else
      file.seek(-search.size, IO::SEEK_CUR)
    end
  end
end
```

Finally, you might want to walk through a file in *groups of bytes*. You would do this on general binary data, where the contents aren't necessarily text at all. For instance, you might want to read the last *N* bytes of information from a file to access metadata information. Let's make up a metadata format: a 120-byte section that is appended to a file; it has five 24-byte fields.

```
File.open('mydata.bin', 'r') do |file|
  file.seek(-120, IO::SEEK_END)  while chunk =
file.read(24)    # examine chunk for data
  end
end
```

In practice, though, it would be easier to just read in all 120 bytes at once and then #split the resulting String.

When to Use Binary Mode (Win32)

```ruby
File.open 'test.txt', 'r' do |f|
  p f.gets
end

File.open 'test.txt', 'rb' do |f|
  p f.gets
end

# on Linux Ruby 1.8.4 produces:
"Hello world!\r\n"
"Hello world!\r\n"

# on Windows Ruby 1.8.4 produces
"Hello World!\n"
"Hello world!\r\n"
```

Our friends from the Windows world need to pay special attention to this section (although it wouldn't hurt for Unix users to pay attention as b is ignored on those platforms).

The b option, which may be passed to File.open, allows special processing of line endings on the Windows platform. As I mention in Chapter 2 "Working with Strings," lines end in \n on *nix, and lines end in \r\n on Windows.

In Windows, Ruby transparently converts any line endings that it finds to the \n form. This can be troublesome for applications on Windows that expect \r\n to be there. By reading and writing files in b binary mode, you ensure that the Windows-specific line endings are maintained.

Obtaining an Exclusive Lock

```
File.open '/tmp/myscript-lock',
File::CREAT|File::TRUNC|File::WRONLY do |lockfile|
  if lockfile.flock(File::LOCK_EX|File::LOCK_NB) ==
0
    # do stuff
  end
end
```

The code at #do stuff works only if an exclusive lock
("cooperative lock") on the file can be obtained. This
is a convenient way to create a Ruby daemon that can
run periodically to perform maintenance and adminis-
trative tasks. If the periodic program executor (cron in
UNIX-like, scheduler in Win32) tries to start another
instance of this script while a previous copy is
running, it simply exits. If this script aborts or crashes
for any reason, the OS's kernel removes the lock automatically.

Copying, Moving, and Deleting Files

```
# create directory
mkdir(directory, options)

# remove directory
rmdir(directory, options)

# copy file, copy directory recursively
cp(source, destination, options)
cp_r(source, destination, options)

# move file
mv(source, destination, options)

# remove file, recursively, or recursively with
```

```
force
rm(list, options)
rm_r(list, options)
rm_rf(list, options)
```

You can perform file operations within Ruby using
the FileUtils module. This module enables you to do
most file operations without calling an external program. It has the added benefit of providing some
meaningful error processing. You can do each of these
file operations relative to the current directory. To find
out what the current directory is, use FileUtils.pwd; to
change the directory, use FileUtils.cd.

The options parameter to these methods is a Hash that
is expected to have one or more of the following *keys:*

```
:force # force overwrite; suppress error on rm
:noop # don't actually do anything, just
 # pretend
:preserve # preserve permissions
:verbose # display information about what is being
 # done
```

As an alternative you can "include FileUtils::Verbose"
when you're trying to debug, and then remove the
"::Verbose" when you're ready to go into production,
as opposed to putting :verbose in every call.

For example, here's a method I might have used used a
lot while writing this book:

```
FileUtils.cp_r 'Book', 'Book Backup', :force => true
```

If you are on *nix, you'll find a lot of other helpful
methods in FileUtils. See Ruby's "ri FileUtils" for
documentation on those methods.

7

Manipulating Text

Of all the things Ruby does, it manipulates text the best. And why shouldn't it? It's great at working with pipes and gluing stuff together. The following code snippets give some good examples of places where text manipulation is critical for system administration.

Parsing an LDIF

```
current_entry = {}
all_entries = []
file = File.open 'test.ldif'

file.each_line do |line|
  if line[0,1] == ' ' or line[0,1] == "\t"
    current_entry[$1] += line.chomp[1..-1]
  else
    /(.+): (.+)/ =~ line
    if ( $1 == nil and $2 == nil )
      all_entries.push current_entry.dup unless
current_entry == {}
      current_entry = {}
    else
      current_entry[$1] = $2
    end
  end
end

p all_entries
```

LDIF is a plain-text file format used to store information about an LDAP tree. LDIF is particularly frustrating to parse because of a feature that allows a continuation of the current line of syntax on the next line, but *only* if the following line starts with a space or a *tab*.

This example takes test.1dif and generates an Array of Hashes. Each Hash represents an LDIF entry. LDIF files generally look something like this:

```
dn: footastic
test: something
foobar: line continuation with a
        tab
foobaz: line continuation with a
 space

dn: baztar
test: something2
baztar: line continuation with a
   tab
baztag: line continuation with a
 space
```

Parsing a Simple Config File

```
require 'pp'

config = {}
config["globals"] = {}
insert_point = "globals"
while gets do
  if $_.match /\[(.+?)\]/
    insert_point = $1
    config[insert_point] = {}
  elsif $_.match /(.+?)=(.+)/
    config[insert_point][$1.strip] = $2.strip
  end
end

pp config
```

This code produces the following output:

```
{"stanza1"=>{"stanza1 var"=>"boo"},
 "stanza2"=>{"stanza2 var"=>"baz"},
 "globals"=>{"a global var"=>"foobar"}}
```

A popular format for config files is to have key = value pairs in a file, one per line, sometimes even with [stanzas]. The previous code implements a simple parser for that format using the Regexp engine to determine syntax in the input file.

Here is the config file that was input:

```
a global var = foobar

[stanza1]
stanza1 var = boo

[stanza2]
stanza2 var = baz
```

Interpolating One Text File into Another

```ruby
config = {'a global var' => 'foobar'}

str = File.read('template.txt')

config.keys.each do |key|
  str.gsub! "%#{key}%", config[key]
end

File.open('template.txt', 'w') do |f|
  f.write str
end
```

We can open a file and replace any %variablename% occurrences based on the values that exist in a Hash called config. Let's look at this as an extension of the previous section; say that you had a template file that looked like this:

```
This is some template text. One of the variables
collected from the file we parsed was called
"a global var" and it's value was %a global var%.
```

This code will use the values stored in `config` and replace %a global var% with the value "foobar".

Sorting the Contents of a File

```
File.open 'file.txt', 'w' do |file|
  file.write(
File.read('file.txt').split("\n").sort.join )
end
```

Although this code is short and sweet, if you'd like to sort by some other criteria, you can use the &block parameter to #sort to change the behavior. For instance, to sort the file by the third text column in a CSV, you would do this:

```
File.open 'file.txt', 'w' do |file|
  ary = File.read('file.txt').split("\n")
  ary.sort! { |a,b| a.split(',')[2] <=>
b.split(',')[2] }
  file.write( ary.join )
end
```

Processing a passwd File

```ruby
attr_accessor :user, :uid, :gid,
 :fullname, :home, :shell
 def initialize(user, uid, gid, fullname,
 home, shell)
 @user, @uid, @gid, @fullname, @home, @shell =
 user, uid, gid, fullname, home, shell
 end
 def passwd_entry
 [@user,@uid,@gid,
 @fullname,@home,@shell].join ':'
  end
end

ary = []

File.open('/etc/passwd', 'r') do |file|
  file.each do |line|
    tmp = line.chomp.split(':').delete_at 1
    ary.push PasswdAccount.new(*tmp)
  end
end
```

This snippet reads this information into your Ruby program with the help of a simple String split. In *nix operating systems, the user account information is stored in a globally readable database at /etc/passwd. For you Windows users, the Apache web server's htpasswd system uses the same format.

To update an account, you can simply walk to the line you want to replace and write this:

```ruby
ary[0].passwd_entry
  #=> "root:0:0:root:/root:/bin/bash"
```

8

Ruby One-Liners

You might be asking yourself, "Why one-liners?" To the bearded UNIX guru, it is obvious that each of these examples can be accomplished (and perhaps improved) with simple bash, grep, sed, or awk commands. However, the motivation for this section is twofold: Our readers from the Windows world will find that those programs aren't available for their platform unless they install something like Cygwin. In addition, most of us mere mortals cannot remember all the semantics for several programming languages 100% of the time. For the programmer and system administrator who swim in Ruby most of the time, it is nice to be able to use knowledge you already have to solve everyday issues. Besides, one-liners are fun!

In Chapter 5, "Working with Pipes," I demonstrated that anything that outputs to STDOUT can be used in a pipe chain. Any of the following examples that take a filename parameter can also be used in a pipe chain.

Note: If you have trouble getting these examples to work on your operating system, try inverting the quotes (change " to ' and vice versa).

Simple Search

```
ruby -n -e 'print "LINE #{$.}: #{$_}" if /Jason/i'\
public_html/index.html
```

This is an example of searching an HTML file for occurrences of a particular string and outputting a LINE #: prefix as well as the matching line.

Notice that I used //i to set the search to non-case-sensitive.

This code produces the following output:

```
LINE 7: <title>mail.jasonclinton.com</title>
LINE 11: <h2>About mail.jasonclinton.com</h2>
LINE 15: <p>If you need to contact this server's ...
```

Counting Lines in a File

```
ruby -n -e 'END { p $. }' public_html/index.html
```

You can do this one in many ways, but this method is the smallest. This works because $. records the number of lines read in. And END {} is always executed before a script exits. This particular code, when run on the file I use later in the chapter "Processing XML", produces a value of 19.

Head or Tail of a File

```
ruby -p -e 'exit 0 if $. > 3' public_html/index.html
```

head (show the first N lines of a file) is rather simple. It produces the following output:

```
<?xml version="1.0"?>
<!DOCTYPE html PUBLIC "-//W3C//DTD XHTML 1.0  ...
```

```
"http://www.w3.org/TR/xhtml1/DTD/xhtml1-transi-
tional.dtd">
```

But `tail` is a bit more nasty. There's no easy way to walk backward through a file from the end. The shortest thing to do is to read the whole file, keeping only the last *N* lines. This version shows only the last five lines:

```
ruby -e 'a=[]; while gets; a.push $_; \
a.shift if $.> 5; end; a.each{|e| print e}' \
public_html/index.html
```

This code produces the following output:

```
<p>If you need to contact this server's ...

</body>
</html>
```

*(blank line)*However, a much better and faster implementation uses the operating system's file-seek methods to intelligently jump to the end of the file. It can be found in the experimental module called `file-tail` available in the *Ruby Application Archives*. Here is a sample of using this module:

```
require 'file/tail'
# ...
File::Tail::Logfile.open ('public_html/index.html')
do |file|
  file.rewind(5).tail { |line| puts line }
end
```

MD5 or SHA1 Hash

```
ruby -0777 -n -r md5 -e 'puts MD5.new($_).\
hexdigest' public_html/index.html
```

This code produces the following output:

```
879d890e2c45582ae0bdb5d2749351a4
```

MD5 is becoming less common, but many websites still use it to verify that you downloaded a file correctly.

However, it's not very secure these days . Some people are moving to SHA1:

```
ruby -0777 -n -r sha1 -e 'puts\
SHA1.new($_).hexdigest' public_html/index.html
```

This code produces the following output:

```
18c9b79fc87cec2596b1a608dd6e3b3680615f2a
```

Also, watch out: This command reads the entire file into RAM to calculate the hash (not particularly handy when hashing ISOs). If you want to avoid this caveat, check out the "Encrypting a String" subsection in Chapter 2 "Working with Strings".

But if you're looking for something really secure, you should be using some kind of public-key cryptography (such as GnuPG or PGP).

Simple HTTP Fetch

```
ruby -rnet/http -e 'Net::HTTP.new\
("mail.jasonclinton.com").request_get\
("/index.html") {|r| r.read_body { |s| print s } }'
```

Imagine that you didn't have something like wget available. This version is a bit longer than it could be, but it enables you to download very large files because it saves the results in chunks and prints the fetched file to STDOUT. You can save it to a file using a Ruby method or just use the shell > operator to save it to a file:

```
ruby -rnet/http -e 'Net::HTTP.new\
("mail.jasonclinton.com").request_get\
("/index.html") {|r| r.read_body{ |s| print s } }' \
> index.html
```

Simple TCP Connect

```
ruby -rsocket -e 'TCPSocket.new("localhost", 80)'
```

The previous command helps if you want to see whether a socket is open on a host—"Is there a web server running?" I primarily use the telnet command for this, but sometimes I find myself on a system that doesn't have it (such as some web hosts where I don't have administrator rights).

You can also embed this command in a shell script to test for a remote service state. If the remote service is not up, it throws an unhandled exception, which results in a nonzero return value (making it "false").

Escaping HTML

```
ruby -0777 -n -rcgi -e 'print CGI.escapeHTML($_)'\
public_html/index.html
```

This command escapes an HTML example so you can put it on a web page without affecting the layout (that is, it appears as plain text). This is also good to keep in mind when working with user-submitted content on your website.

This code produces the following output:

```
...
&lt;h2&gt;About jasonclinton.com&lt;/h2&gt;
...
```

Deleting Empty Directories

```
ruby -rfileutils -rfind -e 'a=[]; Find.find(".") \
{|p| a.push p }; a.sort.reverse.each \
{ |d|FileUtils.rmdir d rescue Errno::ENOTEMPTY }'
```

This command deletes every empty directory below
the current working directory, recursively. I frequently
use this one on my Music directory.

Hint: The sort.reverse is there to delete the deepest
empty directories first. Since the file system will not
allow us to delete non-empty directories, deleting the
deepest directories first is required.

Adding Users from a Text File

```
ruby -ne 'system("useradd -m #{$1} -g \
#{$3} -G #{$4}") and p("#{$1}:#{$2}") if \
/(.*)\t(.*)\t(.*)\t(.*)/' inputfile.txt | chpasswd
```

Given a file inputfile.txt of the following format:

```
username1  password1  prigrp  auxgrp1,auxgrp2
username2  password2  prigrp  auxgrp1,auxgrp2
...        ...        ...     ...
```

You can merge this file into your *nix passwd database
and create home directories by invoking this one-liner.

Delete All the Files Just Extracted

```
tar vtzf foobar.tar.gz | ruby -rfileutils -e 'a=[];
\
a.push $_.split[5] while gets; a.reverse.each \
{ |f| FileUtils.rm_r f }'
```

The convention for tarballs on UNIX-like systems is to store all the files inside a directory of the same name as the tarball:

```
jclinton@linux:~> tar -tvzf foobar.tar.gz
drwxrwxrwx 1000/1000 0     2005-11-27 16:11:51 foo-
bar/
-rwxr-xr-x 1000/1000 1024 2005-11-27 12:00:00 foo
-rw-r-xr-x 1000/1000 1024 2005-11-27 12:00:00 bar
```

Occasionally, someone forgets that they're supposed to do this and stores the entire archive contents at the top level. If you extract this file into your home directory, for instance, you've suddenly got a mess on your hands. The previous command is a short one-liner to delete everything you just extracted; you could just as easily (and perhaps more safely) replace rm_r with mv to move it to a new directory.

Notice the t option from tar. This outputs the file list instead of extracting it. Again, I use #reverse to do the deepest files first.

9

Processing XML

Among the topics that a programmer will almost certainly encounter, XML is near the top of the list. AJAX has been a key player in bringing awareness of XML (Extensible Markup Language) to the web development industry. With the rabid popularity of *Ruby on Rails*, web developers increasingly need Ruby's support of XML to drive their AJAX user interfaces. In this chapter I'll look at the ways you can use some standard libraries to manipulate XML data.

For this section, I rely on *REXML*, which is currently the most popular XML library for Ruby. However, at the time of this writing, bindings to libxml2 called *libxml-ruby* are under development. By the time you read this, you may find that those bindings are mature enough for production use—check the RAA (http://raa.ruby-lang.org/).

For the rest of this section, I use the following example XML file for demonstration purposes (notice that it's also XHTML):

```
<?xml version="1.0"?>
<!DOCTYPE html
  PUBLIC "-//W3C//DTD XHTML 1.0 Transitional//EN"
  "http://www.w3.org/TR/xhtml1/DTD/xhtml1-transi\
  tional.dtd">
<html xmlns="http://www.w3.org/1999/xhtml">
    <head>
        <title>mail.jasonclinton.com</title>
    </head>
    <body>
        <h2>About mail.jasonclinton.com</h2>
        <p>This server is host to a number of
        projects, all of which are not publicly
        accessible. Perhaps one day I will make
         myself a nice home page on the web.</p>
        <p>If you need to contact this server's
        administrator, just email
        <a href="mailto:root@jasonclinton.com"
        >root@jasonclinton.com</a>.</p>
    </body>
</html>
```

Opening an XML File

```
require 'rexml/document'
file = File.open 'index.xhtml'
myxml = REXML::Document.new file
```

When using REXML, the file is parsed when loading. In the preceding code sample, myxml now contains a REXML::Document object for which parsing has been completed.

We can use REXML::Node#to_s (a superclass of
REXML::Document) to get back a printout of the XML in
the object:

```
puts myxml
```

Using the preceding puts statement creates the following—abbreviated for space—output:

```
<?xml version='1.0'?>
<!DOCTYPE html PUBLIC "-//W3C//DTD ...
<html xmlns='http://www.w3.org/1999/xhtml'>
<head>
<title>mail.jasonclinton.com</title>
...
```

Accessing an Element (Node)

```
myxml.root
        #=> <html xmlns='http://www.w3.org/1999/
xhtml'> ... </>
```

As shown in the preceding code sample, myxml has only
one child, the root of the parse tree. You can also
access the children of any node by using the elements
member:

```
myxml.elements.each { |elem| puts elem.name }
```

When evaluated, the preceding statement produces on
STDOUT

```
html
```

Beneath the root, lies the rest of the parse tree:

```
myxml.root.elements.each { |elem| puts elem.name }
```

The use of elements here is one level lower than the earlier example. This lower level produces

```
head
body
```

After you have your REXML::Document object (such as one returned by the code in the section "Opening an XML File," earlier in the chapter), you can access the elements a number of ways. I access the root of the parse tree, <html> in this case, using #root. You can also access an Elements object, which contains access to all children of the element. In the previous example I showed this by accessing the root element and then iterating over its children with #elements#each.

Note that REXML::Document is a special version of an Element; it behaves like a Parent but does not have attributes like an Element. So, you can access its children but not any siblings or its parent (as should be expected).

Elements can be accessed by XPath, yielding all elements that match the path:

```
myxml.each_element('html/body/p') { |elem| puts elem
}
```

The evaluation of #each_element's block produces the following output due to the presence of two paragraphs (p) in the index.xhtml document:

```
<p>This server is host to a number of projects …
<p>If you need to contact this server's admin …
```

Or, you can single out the element by its order (such as I show here using the [2]):

```
myxml.elements['html/body/p[2]/a']
   #=> <a href='mailto:root@jasonclinton.com'> …
```

The most powerful feature for finding a node is the XPath support shown in the preceding example. For those new to XML, XPath is a specification for pointing to a location in an XML tree. For instance, html/body/p points to any paragraphs (<p>) in the <body> of my example file.

You can also use the XPath support to access the first element that matches. In the previous example, I specifically ask for the second paragraph by using a [2]. If there were more than one <a> in that paragraph, only the first would return.

Getting a List of Attributes

```
myxml.elements['//a'].attributes.each do |attr, val|
      p attr, val
end
```

Evaluating the preceding code block with the XPath set to //a produces

```
"href"
"mailto:root@jasonclinton.com"
```

The method REXML::Element#attributes returns an Attributes object, which has a number of helpful methods we can use. To obtain a complete list of all attributes of the element, we can use the #each method. In the preceding example, for instance, I can access all the <a>'s in the document.

We can also access a specific attribute such as a Hash
(Attributes is a subclass of Hash):

```
myxml.elements['//a'].attributes['href']
       #=> "mailto:root@jasonclinton.com"
```

Finally, you can also access the text values (the stuff
between <tag> … </tag>) of an Element:

```
myxml.elements['//a'].text
       #=> root@jasonclinton.com
```

Adding an Element

```
myxml.elements['html/body'].add_element 'p'
       #=> <p/>
```

In XML, if the schema allows it, any node can be a
parent node. For instance, <body> is a node in my
example document. I can add a new <p> node to it as
in the preceding code.

In addition to simply adding a new element, the
#add_element method can also set attributes as it is cre-
ating the element. To do so, pass a block to the
#add_element method.

```
myxml.elements['html/body'].\
    add_element('p', {'id'=>'thanks'}).\
    text = 'Thank you for visiting!'
```

Note that I also changed the enclosed text. This produces the following:

```
<?xml version='1.0'?><!DOCTYPE html PUBLIC "-
//W3C//DTD …
<html xmlns='http://www.w3.org/1999/xhtml'>
<head>
<title>mail.jasonclinton.com</title>
</head>
<body>
<h2>About mail.jasonclinton.com</h2>
<p>This server is host to a number of projects ...
<p>If you need to contact this server's admin ...
<p id='thanks'>Thank you for visiting!</p>
</body>
</html>
```

Changing an Element's Enclosed Text

```
myxml.elements['html/body/p[3]'].add_text ' '
myxml.elements['html/body/p[3]'].add_element('a',
        {'href'=>'/'}).text = 'Home'
myxml.elements['html/body/p[3]'].\
    add_text ' Come again!'
print myxml.to_s
```

Again using an Xpath pointer, the preceding code
sample produces an REXML object containing the
following text:

```
<p id='thanks'>Thank you for visiting!
    <a href='/'>Home</a> Come again!</p>
…
```

The preceding code could be executed on the node
added in the previous section "Adding an Element."

You can add more text, or elements, at any time by using the #add_text and #add_element methods.

Deleting an Element

```
myxml.delete_element 'html/body/p[2]/a'

    # is equivalent to

myxml.elements['html/body/p[2]'].delete_element 'a'
```

Either of the preceding statements results in the following output:

```
<p>If you need to contact this server's
    administrator, just email .</p>
...
```

You can delete elements by using the XPath specification for the node that you want to remove. There are two ways to do this: from the REXML::Document object or from any ::Element object. Both ways use the #delete_element method.

The difference between the two forms is that Element objects are limited to deleting only children of themselves.

Adding an Attribute

```
myxml.elements['html/body/p[2]/a'].add_attribute(
    'id', 'emaillink')
```

Again, using the XPath specification to indicate the point of interest produces the following output:

```
...:root@jasonclinton.com' id='emaillink'>root@jasonc...
```

As you can see, adding attributes to existing nodes is simple.

Changing an Attribute

```
myxml.elements['html/body/p[2]/a'].\
    attributes['id'] = 'somelink'
```

The preceding evaluates to the following #to_s representation:

```
...:root@jasonclinton.com'
id='somelink'>root@jasonc...
Likewise, changing an attribute is just as easy.
```

Deleting an Attribute

```
myxml.elements['html/body/p[2]/a'].\
    delete_attribute 'id'
```

Evaluates to:

```
...:root@jasonclinton.com'>root@jasonc...
```

The preceding code should not be surprising given the previous two examples; deleting is easy too.

Escaping Characters for XML

```
require 'rexml/document'
myxml = REXML::Document.new
myxml.add_element 'rootnode'
myxml.root.text = '<<illegal characters>>'
puts myxml.to_s
```

Produces

```
<rootnode>&lt;&lt;illegal characters&gt;&gt;
</rootnode>
```

Escaped characters in XML are called *entity references*, and they start with an ampersand (&) and end with a semicolon (;). When using the REXML::Document#write and #to_s methods, REXML automatically replaces any strings that must be escaped that it finds in text or attribute values.

Transforming Using XSLT

```
require 'xml/xslt'
xslt = XML::XSLT.new
xslt.xml = "index.xhtml"
xslt.xsl = "index.xsl"
print xslt.serve
```

REXML is just an XML parser and builder—it doesn't know anything about XSLT. To use XSLT, which itself is a language stored in XML, you'll need another tool. One such tool is the ruby-xslt module. This module is a binding to libxslt, a member of the same family as libxml2 (which I discuss in *Validating Your XML*). Using ruby-xslt, we can perform operations without using any other modules.

Let's say that I want to convert my XHTML file into something more generic. XHTML is a large specification; perhaps I am only interested in having a simple "document with paragraphs and links" XML format.

Again, I use the sample XHTML file from the beginning of this chapter. The code sample at the beginning of this section makes use of the following sample XSLT file:

```
<?xml version="1.0" ?>
<xsl:stylesheet
    xmlns:xsl="http://www.w3.org/1999/XSL/Transform"
    version="1.0">
<xsl:template match="/">
    <xsl:element name="document">
        <xsl:element name="title">
            <xsl:value-of select="html/head/title"
/>
        </xsl:element>

        <xsl:element name="body">
            <xsl:for-each select="html/body/p">
                <paragraph>
                    <xsl:apply-templates />
                </paragraph>
            </xsl:for-each>
        </xsl:element>
    </xsl:element>
</xsl:template>
<xsl:template match="a">
    <xsl:element name="link">
        <xsl:apply-templates />
    </xsl:element>
</xsl:template>
</xsl:stylesheet>
```

Obviously, the preceding XSLT might as well be Egyptian hieroglyphs to anyone not familiar with the

XSLT language. If you are interested in learning XSLT, consider checking out the W3C's website for XSLT (http://www.w3.org/TR/xslt/).

The simple set of Ruby code at the beginning of the section executes the actual XSLT processing. When run, it produces the following (reformatted for readability):

```
<?xml version="1.0"?>
<document>
    <title>mail.jasonclinton.com</title>
    <body>
        <paragraph>This server is host to a number
        of projects, all of which are not publicly
        accessible. Perhaps one day I will make
        myself a nice home page on the
        web.</paragraph>

        <paragraph>If you need to contact this
        server's administrator, just email
        <link>root@jasonclinton.com</link>.
        </paragraph>
    </body>
</document>
```

Validating Your XML

```
#!/usr/bin/ruby
require 'xml/libxml'
XML::Parser::default_validity_checking = true
myxml = XML::Document.file "index.xhtml"
```

At the time of this writing, REXML has a partially functional XML validator based on relax-ng. However, because it is not complete, I can't discuss what the final method calls might look like. In the meantime you might want to experiment with the newly available release of libxml-ruby, the bindings to Gnome's libxml2. The preceding code samples from this chapter validate using that library.

This works because a `<DOCTYPE … />` definition is in the beginning of the example document I included at the beginning of this section. libxml2 automatically goes to w3c.org and fetches the needed definitions for validation (this works as of version 0.3.4). Alternatively, you can place the needed definitions in /etc/xml. You can turn off this fetching behavior with

```
XML::Parser::default_load_external_dtd = false
```

Version 0.3.6 of libxml-ruby will include the capability to use #validate(XML::DTD) on any XML::Document object—even after it has been loaded. However, at the time of this writing there is no way to obtain the DTD (Doctype Definition) from the XML::Document object. Instead, you must find the DTD by opening the file and locating it. By the time you read this, the access to the DTD or schema will most likely be implemented. See the libxml-ruby documentation on RubyForge to find out what that method has been named.

A Simple RSS Parser

```
#!/usr/bin/ruby
require 'net/http'
require 'rexml/document'
http = Net::HTTP.new 'www.npr.org'
http.open_timeout = 30
http.start
raise "Connection failed." unless http
```

```
response = http.get('/rss/rss.php?id=1001')
myxml = REXML::Document.new response.body
puts "NPR News Stories"
puts '-----------------------------------------------'
myxml.each_element('rss/channel/item') do |elem|
    puts elem.elements['title'].text
end
```

RSS (Really Simple Subscriptions) is rather like one-way email for new updates. You subscribe to feeds and then browse those feeds using a feed reader. A few months ago, I was playing around with RSS and thought it would be neat to see what the news headlines were by just running a simple script at a terminal. Much to my pleasure, doing something like this in Ruby was simple as the preceding 15 lines of code!

When run, the code produces the following:

```
NPR News Stories
-----------------------------------------------
High-Octane Offenses in Women's Final Four
Despite Alerts, Identity Theft Cases Rise
Thais Vote in Election Meant to Quiet Unrest
Rice, Straw Call for Iraqi Progress; Carroll Is Home
U.S., Allies Discuss Aiding Palestinians, Not Hamas
UCLA, Florida Trounce Lower Seeds to Meet in Final
After Katrina, a Boom in St. Tammany Parish
Confusion Persists as Medicare 'Part D' ...
Thai Elections Held Amid Boycotts
Amid Rallies, Questions Over Immigrants' Impact
Marchers Seek to Delay New Orleans Vote
Prosecutor Preps Taylor Case Amid Venue Doubts
...
```

In plain English: I open up a new HTTP connection
to the NPR server and fetch the feed URL. The
response object stores the result, and the body property
of that object contains the text XML that we want to
parse. I pass the XML to `REXML::Document#new` and just
use a simple `#each_element` method to walk over all the
`<title>` elements. It's that simple!

## 10

Rapid Applications Development with GUI Toolkits

In the world of Ruby GUI toolkit bindings, two high-quality cross-platform options are available: GTK+ 2.x and Qt 4 (pronounced *cute*). Both of these toolkits provide a consistent experience across Linux, Win32, and Mac OS 10+ as well as have stable APIs and support for antialiased text on the Linux platform. The largest difference between the two is the license. GTK+ is LGPL, which means that you can develop proprietary or other-licensed source programs with it.

Qt is *triple licensed*: By default you get either the GPL or the QPL license, which both require that the program you develop be completely open source; that is, not proprietary, closed source distribution. However, for a fee, Trolltech, the company that makes Qt, will allow you to develop and distribute a proprietary application using the Qt toolkit.

Other than that, the differences are mostly a matter of taste. GTK+ is written in C; Qt in C++.

The Fox and Tk toolkits are also handy if you want to hack something up quickly on the Windows platform. However, they both look ugly on Linux.

In this chapter, I'll show you both GTK+ and Qt.

A Simple GTK+ Hello World

```
require 'gtk2'
Gtk.init
vbox = Gtk::VBox.new 2
button = Gtk::Button.new 'Hello World'
entry = Gtk::Entry.new
entry.text = 'Hello?'
window = Gtk::Window.new 'A Hello World App.'
window.border_width = 5
window.add vbox
vbox.pack_start button
vbox.pack_start entry
window.show_all
Gtk.main
```

Before you can run the preceding code sample, you first need to install the Ruby Gnome2 bindings by either visiting its website at <http://ruby-gnome2.sourceforge.jp/> or using your Linux distribution's package manager. On a Debian-based system, the package is ruby-gnome2.

The preceding code generates a window that looks like that shown in Figure 10.1.

Figure 10.1   Simple Hello World window.

The preceding code is simple. We call Gtk#init, which parses some of the standard GTK+ command-line options and does some housekeeping. Then, we declare four objects, which in turn correspond to four visual objects (*widgets*) on the screen: a window, a button, an entry box, and a special kind of box called a VBox. A VBox can be thought of as a container widget for other widgets. We "add" the VBox object to the window, and in turn ask the VBox to start "packing" widgets in to its vertical stack. We tell GTK+ to show the window (windows can exist but be hidden). Finally, we activate GTK+'s main loop. #main is a binding to the C function of the same name. While inside #main, GTK+ waits for events to occur (such as an uncover event or a mouse click or movement). When events are received, certain actions are taken.

There's a problem, though. You can close the window, but the Ruby application never exits from the Gtk#main method call (you have to press Ctrl+C at the shell to break out). Also, the button doesn't work. So let's attach some code. Code that can be called by #main is called a *callback*.

```
require 'gtk2'
Gtk.init
vbox = Gtk::VBox.new 2
button = Gtk::Button.new 'Hello World'
entry = Gtk::Entry.new
entry.text = 'Hello?'
window = Gtk::Window.new 'A Hello World App.'
window.border_width = 5
window.add vbox
vbox.pack_start button
vbox.pack_start entry
window.show_all
```

```
window.signal_connect("destroy") do
        Gtk.main_quit
end
button.signal_connect("clicked") do
        entry.text = 'Hello! Hello!'
end
Gtk.main
```

And now it works! The result is show in Figure 10.2.

Figure 10.2 Window showing entry with new next.

Using Glade

```
$ ruby-glade-create-template helloworld.glade >
helloworld.rb
```

Making applications using the direct GTK+ method can be tedious, especially if you have a complex window. Instead, you can design your application in the Glade UI Designer and then have GTK+ automatically create all your widgets and their associated Ruby objects. Glade creates an XML file; we simply load this XML file into our Ruby application, and all the magic happens! Let's look at the Glade equivalent of the example from GTK+ section.

After starting up Glade, click the New button and select GTK+ Project. Then, begin by creating a new window by clicking the Window button. A new blank window like the one shown in Figure 10.3 appears.

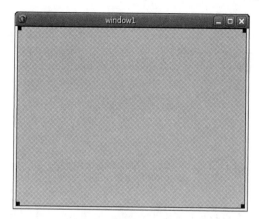

Figure 10.3   A blank Glade window.

Next, add the VBox container by clicking the Vertical Box button and clicking in the checkerboard area in the new, blank window. Specify that you want two rows, and you should now see a split region as shown in Figure 10.4.

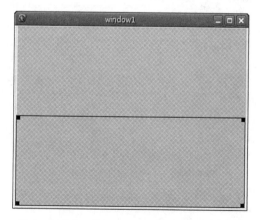

Figure 10.4   Glade window area split in two.

Next, click the Button button and click on the upper region to insert it. And finally, click on the Entry button and click on the lower region to insert it. After resizing the window, it should look like Figure 10.5.

Figure 10.5   Glade window with button and entry field.

Now, there are a few housekeeping things to do. Use the mouse cursor to select the button. In the Properties window, on the Widget tab, give the button a meaningful name such as "hello_button" and set the button text to "Hello World".

Figure 10.6   Glade properties window.

Do the same for the entry field in the lower half of
your window. Click on it and use the Properties window to change its name to "hello_entry". Finally, we
need to give the button a *signal*. (This is different from
a callback. This is a plain text name that is "emitted"
from the widget when an event occurs. Glade checks
your application for a method that can handle it.)
Click on the upper button again and in the Properties
window, go to the Signals tab. Choose Clicked from
the drop-down menu and then click Add to accept the
default signal name suggestion. The window should
look Like Figure 10.7 before you click Add.

Figure 10.7   Glade signals window.

Back in your Ruby application, we just need to do a little magic to make everything work:

```
require 'libglade2'
Gtk.init
def on_hello_button_clicked
    @hello_entry.text = 'Hello! Hello!'
end
@glade = GladeXML.new("/home/jclinton/Projects/pr\
oject1/project1.glade", 'window1') { |handler|
    method(handler)
}
@hello_entry = @glade.get_widget 'hello_entry'
@window1 = @glade.get_widget("window1")
@window1.signal_connect('destroy') {
    Gtk.main_quit
}
Gtk.main
```

You can also use the magic templating program ruby-glade-create-template and run it on your helloworld.glade file. This code is shown at the beginning of this section. The output will be a template Ruby program.

As you can see, it's less tedious to create a GUI interface this way. But it's not a silver bullet. You'll still need to do some manual calls to load items into list views and combo boxes. Some people find that, because you still have to work with the interface manually in some ways, it's just easier to code it directly. Either way, playing with Glade is a good way to get an idea of how GTK+ works and what widgets are available.

A Simple Qt Hello World

```ruby
require 'Qt'
app = Qt::Application.new ARGV
window = Qt::Dialog.new
vgroup = Qt::VBoxLayout.new
button = Qt::PushButton.new -Hello World!-
edit = Qt::LineEdit.new -Hello?-
vgroup.addWidget button
vgroup.addWidget edit
window.setLayout vgroup
window.show
app.exec
```

Before you can run the preceding code, you need to install the Ruby-Qt 4 bindings either by visiting the Korundum website (http://rubyforge.org/projects/korundum/—by the time you read this a binary Win32 installer should be ready) or by using your Linux distribution's package manager to install it. On a Mac, you need to compile the extension from source. Despite its being relatively new, I am using Qt 4 for this section because it is the first release to offer a GPL version on all three platforms.

After executing the previous code, the results should look something like Figure 10.8.

Figure 10.8   Simple Qt Hello World window.

The previous code is simple: We create a new Qt::Application object, which parses the command line for the common Qt options, and allocate a new

Dialog object, which is used as a container for our VBox and its two widgets. To get the VBox to stack the widgets in a column, we add the widgets to the VBox using #addWidget. After everything is allocated, we call the #show method to display the window and then tell the Qt::Application to enter its main event loop with #exec. All in all, not that much different from GTK+.

But, again, just like the GTK+ example, we don't have any functionality. Unlike GTK+, however, we do not need to create a method for destroying this window. So, let's attach some code to the "Hello World!" button.

Attaching a Signal Handler to a Qt Widget Slot

```ruby
require 'Qt'
app = Qt::Application.new ARGV
class MyDialog < Qt::Widget
    slots 'button_clicked()'
    def initialize(parent=nil)
        super(parent)

        @vgroup = Qt::VBoxLayout.new self
        @button = Qt::PushButton.new "Hello World!",
                                      self
        @edit = Qt::LineEdit.new "Hello?", self

        @vgroup.addWidget @button
        @vgroup.addWidget @edit

        connect @button, SIGNAL('clicked()'), self,
        SLOT('button_clicked()')

        self.setLayout @vgroup
    end
    def button_clicked()
```

```
        @edit.text = 'Hello! Hello!'
    end
end
window = MyDialog.new
window.show
app.exec
```

Figure 10.9   A Qt Hello World
that responds to click.

(The principles are the same as in the earlier Qt example, but rather than use Qt::Dialog here, I created my own kind of widget called a MyDialog, which inherits from Qt::Dialog. This subtle change allows me to now attach a few *signal* handlers (called *slots*) using the special methods slots and connect. *slots* tell Qt that the methods in this class by these *names* are special handlers. Other than the use of the slots method, there's nothing special about a method called by a signal. To connect the built-in signal, clicked(), and our own method button_clicked(), we use the special method connect to join the two. This join tells Qt to call the button_clicked() method when the connect signal is emitted.

As a side note, Qt::Object.connect is where the method lives and is a member of all Qt classes because Qt::Object is a super-parent of all Qt classes.

Using Qt Designer

```
$ rbuic -x -o qttest.rb qttest.ui
```

qttest.ui is any file containing a UI definition created by Qt Designer. The output of the *rbuic* program can be tested by running:

```
$ ruby -w qttest.rb
```

Such a test program might output something like Figure 10.10.

Figure 10.10   An example window created by rbuic.

In this example, code in `qttest.ui`, which defines a user interface, was created using handy tool for creating GUI interfaces—a tool provided by Trolltech as a part of Qt. Unlike Glade, the files that describe the interface are interpreted to automatically create C++ headers, but in this case, we want Ruby files. Richard Dale, the author of the Ruby bindings to Qt has provided such a method. But first, let's create the interface for our simple hello world program.

Begin by choosing the Widget option from the New Form dialog (see Figure 10.11).

After doing so, you are presented with the blank working area shown in Figure 10.12.

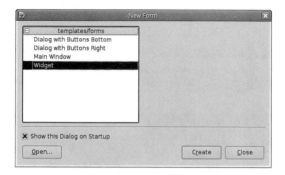

Figure 10.11   The New Form dialog.

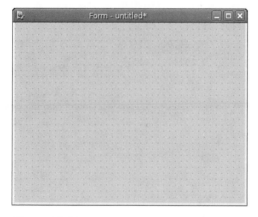

Figure 10.12   Blank working area in Designer.

Now, we need to add some widgets. Let's begin by dragging the Push Button widget from the widget palette at the left onto the blank working area. Do the same for the Line Edit widget. Place the widgets in the general location in which you want them to finally appear. When we do the next step, adding an alignment box, the position that the VBox gives the widgets is influenced by the position that you have placed them in freeform mode.

So let's add that VBox. Right-click in a blank area of the window and choose Lay Out and then Lay Out Vertically, as shown in Figure 10.13.

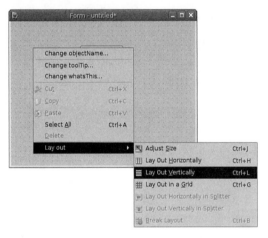

Figure 10.13   Set to vertical layout.

Now, you may want to resize the window to look more like our earlier example.

Let's move on to making these widgets do what we want. We need some names and default text for these widgets. Name each widget using the property editor, as shown in Figure 10.14. Also set the default text for the push button to "Hello World!" and the default text for the line entry to "Hello?".

After making those changes, the designer window should look something like Figure 10.15.

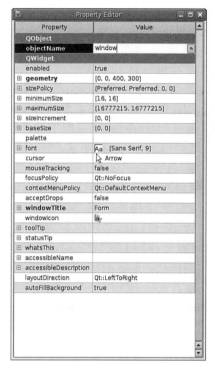

Figure 10.14   Property editor window.

Figure 10.15   Designer area post-changes.

Now, save the .ui file, making a note of where you placed it. It's now time to generate the needed Ruby code by running the code snippet at the beginning of this section.

After running the command at the beginning of this section, a new qttest.rb file is created containing all the code needed to construct the interface. Here are the contents of that generated file (reformatted):

```
require 'Qt'
class Ui_window
    attr_reader :qvboxLayout
    attr_reader :button
    attr_reader :edit
def setupUi(window)
        window.setObjectName("window")
        window.resize(Qt::Size.\
            new(115,78).expandedTo\
            (window.minimumSizeHint()
        ))
        @qvboxLayout = Qt::VBoxLayout.new(window)
        @qvboxLayout.spacing = 6
        @qvboxLayout.margin = 9
        @qvboxLayout.setObjectName("qvboxLayout")
        @button = Qt::PushButton.new(window)
        @button.setObjectName("button")

        @qvboxLayout.addWidget(@button)

        @edit = Qt::LineEdit.new(window)
        @edit.setObjectName("edit")

        @qvboxLayout.addWidget(@edit)

        retranslateUi(window)

        Qt::MetaObject.connectSlotsByName(window)
    end # setupUi
def retranslateUi(window)
        window.setWindowTitle(Qt::Application.\
        translate(
```

```
            "window",
            "Form",
            nil,
            Qt::Application::UnicodeUTF8
        ))
        @button.setText(Qt::Application.translate(
            "window",
            "Hello World!",
            nil,
            Qt::Application::UnicodeUTF8
        ))
        @edit.setText(Qt::Application.translate(
            "window",
            "Hello?",
            nil,
            Qt::Application::UnicodeUTF8
        ))
    end # retranslateUi
end
if $0 == __FILE__
    a = Qt::Application.new(ARGV)
    u = Ui_window.new
    w = Qt::Widget.new
    u.setupUi(w)
    w.show
    a.exec
end
```

You can run it and see what you get.

```
$ ruby -w qttest.rb
```

But it doesn't do anything, yet.

Attaching Signal Handlers to Qt Designer Generated Code

```ruby
require 'Qt'
require 'qttest.rb'
class Form < Qt::Widget
    slots 'on_button_clicked()'

    def initialize(parent = nil)
        super(parent)
        @ui_window = Ui_window.new
        @ui_window.setupUi(self)
    end
    def on_button_clicked()
        @ui_window.edit.setText 'Hello! Hello!'
    end
end
a = Qt::Application.new(ARGV)
f = Form.new
f.show
a.exec
```

The qttest.rb file from the previous section is only able to display itself when run alone. In order to give that file any functionality, we needed to add signal handlers. We want to keep our automatically generated qttest.rb file separate from any code additions that we make so that they are not overwritten if we decide to make changes in the designer. So, I moved the construction code from the end of the qttest.rb file into a new file called main.rb and added the new pushbutton method there. The result was the new main.rb file shown here.

First, we create a new generic Qt::Widget because we need the methods defined here to be accessed by Qt::MetaObject.connectSlotsByName, which can operate only on children of Qt::Object. connectSlotsByName is called from inside the qttest.rb file, which was automatically generated by "rbuic". Examining the automatically generated code in qttest.rb, you'll notice that `connectSlotsByName` is called with the parent class as a parameter (that parent reference was passed in when creating the `Ui_window` instance). For `connectSlotsByName` to do its magic, two things must be true:

- The slot (method) handing an event must be named in this convention:

  `on_<object>_<signal>(<signal params>)`

- The slot must be declared using the `slots` method in the body of the class.

So, in our case, the method `on_button_clicked` follows the required conventions. `button` is the name of the object sending the signal, and `clicked` is the name of the signal.

Run it again using the following command:

```
$ ruby -w main.rb
```

And now our "Hello World" program runs, and the button works as shown in Figure 10.16!

Figure 10.16 Finished Qt Designed window.

## 11

Simple CGI Forms

There are many ways to do CGI with Ruby. For small tasks, I have found that erb/eruby with the cgi module is the simplest, so that's what I use for the rest of this section. The easiest way to get eruby working is to install mod_ruby (and you get a speed boost, to boot!) After mod_ruby is installed, you need to add some code to your Apache configuration to get it interpreting .rhtml files as eruby files.

```
<IfModule mod_ruby.c>
    RubyRequire apache/eruby-run

    <Files *.rhtml>
        SetHandler ruby-object
        RubyHandler Apache::ERubyRun.instance
    </Files>
</IfModule>
```

The preceding code causes Apache to use mod_ruby's special ERubyRun mode to parse any .rhtml file. .rhtml files are similar to ASP or PHP in that they are normal HTML files that contain special <% ... %> clauses that contain executable (Ruby) code.

Processing a Web Form

```
<?xml version="1.0"?>
<!DOCTYPE html PUBLIC "-//W3C//DTD XHTML 1.0 St...
<html xmlns="http://www.w3.org/1999/xhtml">
<head>
<title>process submission</title>
</head>
<body>

<h2>Processing submission:</h2>

<% require 'cgi'; cgi = CGI.new %>

<p>Your message
<blockquote><%= cgi['message'] %></blockquote>
 has been saved to file
<%
  File.open('/tmp/message.txt', 'w') do |f|
    f.write cgi['message']
    print f.path
  end
%>
.</p>

</body>
</html>
```

The preceding code is a simple `submit.rhtml`. This
script takes the browser's request and saves what it
receives to a file on the web server.

Now, when we click the Send button on a separate
page, message.html, the message text is transmitted and
handled by `submit.rhtml` (see Figure 11.1).

This works because the CGI object `cgi` stores a hash
of all `name=` form fields. The rest is just regular Ruby
code. Notice that a special `<%= ... %>` is used that
causes the evaluation of the code inside it to be *interpolated* in to the HTML; otherwise, if we want something to be shown in the rendered web page, we have
to use the `print` or `puts` method calls.

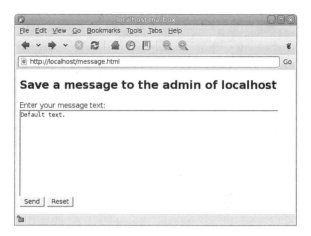

Figure 11.1   Form to submit a message.

Here is a sample HTML form that can be used with the submit.rhtml shown previously:

```
<?xml version="1.0"?>
<!DOCTYPE html PUBLIC "-//W3C//DTD XHTML 1.0 St...
<html xmlns="http://www.w3.org/1999/xhtml">
<head>
<title>localhost mailbox</title>
</head>
<body>

<h2>Save a message to the admin of localhost</h2>

<form method="post" action="cgi-bin/submit.rhtml">
  <div>

    <label for="message">Enter your message
    text:</label><br />
```

```
    <textarea id="message" name="message" rows="10"
    cols="72">Default text.</textarea><br />

    <input type="submit" value="Send" />
    <input type="reset" />

  </div>
</form>

</body>
</html>
```

The important part of this simple message.html file is
which script will process the Send button. To process a
click on the Send button, we just change the action=
property to "submit.rhtml":

```
...
<form method="post" action="cgi-bin/submit.rhtml">
  <div>
...
```

This HTML renders as shown in Figure 11.2.

Of course, the preceding code is of only limited use-
fulness. In production, you would want to either store
such messages in a database or create the filename on a
date time combination (to ensure uniqueness).

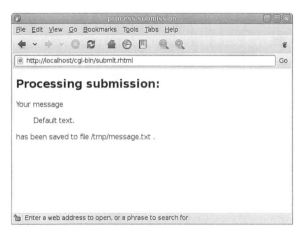

Figure 11.2   Post-processing
message form submit.rhtml.

Returning Tabled Results

```
<?xml version="1.0"?>
<!DOCTYPE html PUBLIC "-//W3C//DTD XHTML 1.0 Str...
<html xmlns="http://www.w3.org/1999/xhtml">
<head>
<title>process submission</title>
</head>
<body>

<h2>Processing submission:</h2>

<% require 'cgi'; cgi = CGI.new %>

<p>We will now display each line of your file
one line at a time:</p>
<table>
<%
  n = 0
  cgi['message'].each_line do |line|
```

```
    n += 1
    print "<tr><th>#{n}</th><td>#{line}</td></tr>"
  end
%>
</table>

</body>
</html>
```

This example demonstrates that you can also loop inside `<% %>` clauses and even generate an infinite amount of HTML from within them—just make sure that you output it using `print` or `puts`.

In the preceding code, we are fetching the named CGI attribute `name=message` from the `CGI` object and then using the `String#each_line` method to iterate over its contents.

To test this code, we can return to our previous sample form and rename it input.html. Make a small modification to the presentation:

```
<?xml version="1.0"?>
<!DOCTYPE html PUBLIC "-//W3C//DTD XHTML 1.0 St...
<html xmlns="http://www.w3.org/1999/xhtml">
<head>
<title>table lines of a file</title>
</head>
<body>

<h2>Iterate by line.</h2>

<form method="post" action="cgi-bin/table.rhtml">
  <div>

    <label for="message">Enter some text to
    iterate one line at a time:</label><br />
```

```
    <textarea id="message" name="message" rows="10"
    cols="72">Default text.</textarea><br />

    <input type="submit" value="Send" />
    <input type="reset" />

  </div>
</form>

</body>
</html>
```

which now displays as shown in Figure 11.3.

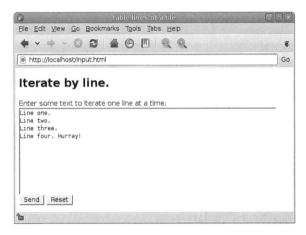

Figure 11.3   Iteration input box.

For our test, we enter the following text in the text field:

```
Line one.
Line two.
Line three.
Line four. Hurray!
```

After clicking Send, our text is rendered by table.rhtml as shown in Figure 11.4.

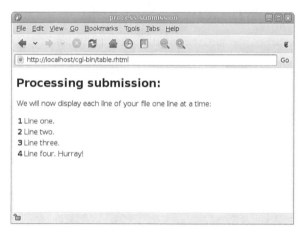

Figure 11.4   Result of iteration.

Escaping Input

```
require 'cgi'
mystring = 'This is some hello/goodbye world text?'

encstring = CGI.escape mystring
  #=> "This+is+some+hello%2Fgoodbye+world+text%3F"

CGI.unescape encstring
  #=> "This is some hello/goodbye world text?"
```

or, for escaping HTML syntax:

```ruby
require 'cgi'
mystring = '<script "scriptkiddie.js" />
 Ow3z0r!</script>'

encstring = CGI.escapeHTML mystring
  #=> "&lt;script &quot;scriptkiddie.js&quot;
    /&gt; Ow3z0r!"

WIth the addition of </script>
  #=> "&lt;script &quot;scriptkiddie.js&quot;
    /&gt; Ow3z0r!&lt;/script&gt;"

CGI.unescapeHTML encstring
  #=> "<script \"scriptkiddie.js\" />
 Ow3z0r!</script>"
```

The CGI module comes with four handy functions for escaping: two for URLs and two for HTML.

URLs cannot contain a number of illegal characters. For instance, "/" and *space* are illegal filenames and also illegal in an HTTP GET-style script query. Your web browser automatically escapes any values provided in form fields when it sends its request to the web server, and CGI automatically converts it back to a normal String on the server side. From time to time, you may find that you need to work with these internal methods directly. This can be done as I have shown previously.

When displaying visitor-created content on your website, to do this safely, you need to convert any occurrences of HTML reserved characters to *entity references* (see Chapter 9, "Processing XML," for more information about these). For example, take the following sample text that you might find on a forum in a dark corner of the Internet; it is stored in the variable mystring:

```ruby
mystring = '<script "scriptkiddie.js" /> Ow3z0r!'
```

Rather than posting this evil code directly to a page, we can escape it so that the HTML references are shown in plain text rather than interpreted by the browser as shown in the code sample at the beginning of this section. This escaped text can be safely transmitted to a browser.

Locking Down Ruby

```
$SAFE = 2 unless $SAFE > 2
```

Ruby has a handy security feature that tracks whether variables are tainted. A *tainted* variable is one that has received its data from some sort of external source (such as a CGI form field or an IO stream) or from copying the contents of another tainted variable. Then certain methods that are considered dangerous will refuse to run if they receive data marked as tainted. These features are turned on and off at varying levels through the use of the $SAFE variable.

$SAFE can be set to level 0 through 4. At level 0, no checks are performed. By default, $SAFE is level 0; however, when using mod_ruby, $SAFE is set to level 1.

$SAFE can be changed inside your program, but it can only be increased. Attempting to decrease it raises an error. It's generally a good idea to start all your .rhtml and CGI .rb files with the line of code at the beginning of this section. At this $SAFE level of "2" Ruby does the following security checks:

- Can't load any file that is in a world-readable directory or whose path starts with "~"—the *nix home directory prefix

- Can't do the following on any `String` marked tainted: `glob`, `eval`, `load`, `require`, `system`, `exec`, and `trap`

- Ignores most Ruby command-line parameters

- Ignores Ruby's environment variables `RUBYOPT` and `RUBYLIB`

- Completely disables most `File` operations having to do with changing and examining permissions, `Process.setpriority`, and the `Process` permissions methods

You can mark data as "untainted" after you have verified that it is valid and safe by using the `Object#untaint` method. Refer to the section "Sanitizing Input" in Chapter 2, "Working with Strings," for code samples that may be useful for validation.

Receiving an Uploaded File

```
<?xml version="1.0"?>
<!DOCTYPE html PUBLIC "-//W3C//DTD XHTML 1.0 St...
<html xmlns="http://www.w3.org/1999/xhtml">
<head>
<title>table lines of a file</title>
</head>
<body>

<% require 'cgi'; require 'time'; cgi = CGI.new
require 'stringio' %>

<h2>Saving file.</h2>

<% uploaded = cgi.params['uploaded'][0] %>

<p>You uploaded <%=uploaded.original_filename%>.</p>

<% File.open(Time.now.iso8601.untaint, 'w') do |f|
```

```
    f << uploaded.read
end %>

<p>Save completed.</p>
</body>
</html>
```

require 'time' is necessary if you want access to Time.now.iso8601

In this example, upload-handler.rhtml, a file is received and the file is written to a file named by the current time. Note that CGI actually uses both Tempfile and StringIO depending on the size of the file upload. Either way, the use of << to direct the contents into our storage file ensures that the received data is copied to its destination.

Untainting the filename of the destination is needed to explicitly tell Ruby that the file path is safe. Otherwise, a security error will be thrown.

A simple HTML form is used to call the upload-handler.rhtml script:

```
<form name='upload' enctype='multipart/form-data'
action='cgi-bin/upload-handler.rhtml' method='post'>
<input type='file' name='uploaded' size='52' />
<input type='submit' value='Upload File' />
</form>
```

Representing Data Graphically

```
<html xmlns="http://www.w3.org/1999/xhtml">
<head>
<title>process submission</title>
</head>
<body>
```

```
<h2>Processing submission:</h2>

<% require 'cgi'; cgi = CGI.new
require 'time'
require 'gnuplot'
%>


<p>Representation of request processing times:</p>


<% data = []
File.open('/tmp/times.txt', 'r') do |f|
    f.each_line do |line|
        data.push line.to_f
    end
end

plotcmd = ''
Gnuplot::Plot.new(plotcmd) do |plot|
        plot.add_data Gnuplot::DataSet.new(data)
        plot.terminal 'svg'
end

IO.popen(Gnuplot.gnuplot, 'w+') do |gp|
    gp.write plotcmd
    gp.close_write
    3.times{ gp.readline }
    print gp.read
end %>


<p>
<% time = Time.now - Apache.request.request_time;
puts "This request took #{time}. Added to end of
record."%>
</p>

<% File.open('/tmp/times.txt', 'a+') do |f|
    f.puts time
end %>


</body>
</html>
```

In the preceding code sample, I use the Gnuplot (http://www.gnuplot.info/)"Ruby bindings to plot a chart of the amount of time it takes to process each request. At the end of the page load, I add the current processing time to the end of /tmp/times.txt as a simple way to tabulate the data (rrdtool would be a better way).

NOTE: rrdtool is an efficient disk-format database for storing time-related statistics. For example, if you wanted to always keep the last 24 hours of network activity in a database that never grows in size, rrdtool would provide a very efficient means by which to store that data. The most recent version even provides some graphing facilities.

The Gnuplot bindings are somewhat confusing. In the preceding code sample, the plotcmd variable is used by Gnuplot::Plot as a kind of buffer to store the full list of instructions for Gnuplot. The bindings *only* allow for the use of its methods with code blocks.

The line 3.times is used to eliminate the DOCTYPE declaration from the front of Gnuplot's output before it is incorporated into the body of the HTML.

Control over the size of the plot area can be adjusted by providing parameters to the terminal method. At a command prompt enter the following command to access Gnuplot's parameters:

```
gnuplot> help svg
```

Pay special attention to the way the file is delivered to the browser: a MIME type of `application/xml` is required. You can accomplish this by changing the following code to your Apache configuration:

```
AddType application/xml .rhtml
```

Alternatively, you can send `Content-Type: application/xml` in the response headers.

Also alternatively, `Gnuplot` can output to PNG. In this case, a separate script could be provided as the `src=` of an `img` tag: the `STDOUT` of `Gnuplot` would contain the data stream. Or, `Tempfile` could be used and then deleted after some amount of time has elapsed (24 hours, for example).

For the preceding example, I output the `Gnuplot` data to SVG and incorporate the SVG markup into the HTML. This is rendered as shown in Figure 11.5.

Note that Internet Explorer doesn't support native display of SVG.

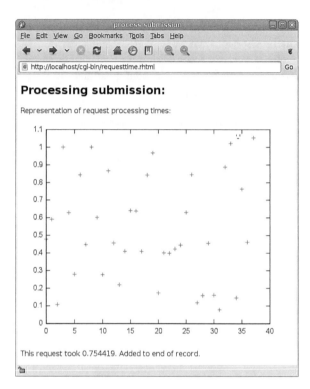

Figure 11.5   Rendering of plot data in browser.

## 12

Connecting to Databases

I selected MySQL for this chapter because it is available and well-supported on all platforms. Two other databases that you might consider are PostgreSQL and SQLite. Both are fine database systems, and I would encourage you to consider them as options before you settle on MySQL. In all the examples in this chapter, a DBD (database driver) other than mysql could be substituted and used in the same way. At the time of this writing there are 13 available database drivers: ADO, DB2, Frontbase, InterBase, mSQL, MySQL, ODBC, Oracle, OCI8, Pg, Proxy, SQLite, and SQLRelay (see Ruby DBI Documentation, http://ruby-dbi. rubyforge.org/).

Ruby's MySQL bindings come in either the direct flavor or the DBI (database interface) flavor. DBI insulates the programmer from some of the specifics of database systems, thereby making it easier to switch between them. For this chapter, the DBI bindings are discussed.

Opening (and Closing) a MySQL Database Connection

```
require 'dbi'
DBI.connect('dbi:mysql:test:localhost',
    'user', 'pass') do | handler |
    # do stuff ...
end
```

The preceding code merely creates a connection to the MySQL server and yields it to the handler object. The dbi:Mysql signifies that the DBI should search for and load the Ruby MySQL DBI driver. test is the name of the database (or *schema*), and localhost is the hostname (or IP address) of the server. When the code block ends, handler will be closed automatically. Alternatively, you may assign the connection to an explicit object, which must be manually closed.

```
handler = DBI.connect('dbi:Mysql:test:localhost',
    'user', 'pass')
```

Such a handler object can be explicitly closed by issuing a single method call:

```
handler.disconnect
```

In all the following code samples, I use a handler object to refer to the connection to the database server.

For this chapter, assume that we are writing a web application called *Vegetable Tracker*.

Creating a Table

```ruby
require 'dbi'
DBI.connect('dbi:mysql:test:localhost', 'root',
    'password') do | handler |
    query =  <<-QUERY
        CREATE TABLE `vegetables` (
            `ID` INT( 8 ) NOT NULL AUTO_INCREMENT
            PRIMARY KEY ,
            `type` VARCHAR( 255 ) NOT NULL ,
            `vendor` VARCHAR( 255 ) NOT NULL
        ) ENGINE = MYISAM ;
    QUERY
    handler.do(query)
end
```

Here, we are merely executing MySQL statements
inside a DBI#connect code block on an existing handler
object. The preceding MySQL syntax creates a table of
vegetables that will be used in the following code samples. Notice that a HEREDOC (the <<-QUERY starts the
HEREDOC) is used to format the code to make it
more readable. HEREDOCs are a great way to
increase the legibility of nested SQL syntax. When
using HEREDOCs, be sure to insert the needed "-" in
front of the WORD you would like to use as a delim-
iter. This causes Ruby to allow you to stop your
HEREDOC on an indented line.

See the section "Catching Errors" later in the chapter
for a discussion of what happens when a table already
exists.

Getting a List of Tables

```
require 'dbi'
DBI.connect('dbi:mysql:test:localhost', 'root',
    'password') do | handler |
    handler.select_all('SHOW TABLES') do | tables |
        p tables
    end
end
```

The list of tables is returned as one-element arrays, one at a time. The preceding code produces the following:

```
["vegetables"]
["vendors"]
```

Adding Rows to a Table

```
require 'dbi'
DBI.connect('dbi:mysql:test:localhost', 'root',
    'password') do | handler |
    %w{ carrots corn artichokes }.each do |veg|
        query = 'insert into vegetables (type)
            VALUES (?)'
        handler.do(query, veg)
    end
end
```

For adding rows to existing tables, again, the handler.do() method is used. DBI allows for interpolation in the form of a "?" positional notation. Any additional arguments to #do are interpolated into ?'s in order in the query string provided as the first argument.

Iterating Over Queried Rows

```
require 'dbi'
DBI.connect('dbi:mysql:test:localhost', 'root',
'password') do | handler |
        handler.select_all\
        ('select * from vegetables') do |row|
                p row
        end
end
```

The object row contains a one-dimensional array containing values. This example is almost identical to the
example in the "Getting a List of Tables" section earlier
in the chapter. Here is what is produced:

```
[1, "carrots", ""]
[2, "corn", ""]
[3, "artichokes", ""]
```

Notice that MySQL automatically incremented the ID
column just as we would expect (because of the previous table definition).

Deleting Rows

```
DBI.connect('dbi:mysql:test:localhost', 'root',
'password') do | handler |
        handler.do("DELETE FROM `vegetables`\
        WHERE `ID` =2 LIMIT 1 ; ")
end
```

Continuing a theme, the significant point of variance
here is the MySQL syntax.

However, there is one important difference between
this code sample and the others in this section: If the
data that you request to be deleted isn't already there,
you will not receive any kind of different return value,
and no exception object will be raised. Keep this in
mind when writing your application's logic.

Deleting a Table

```
require 'dbi'
DBI.connect('dbi:mysql:test:localhost', 'root',
'password') do | handler |
        handler.do('DROP TABLE `vegetables`')
end
```

And finally, like almost all of the previous examples,
#do is used to accomplish the table deletion. Note,
however, that unlike deleting a row, deleting a table
that does not exist *will* throw an exception such as this:

```
in `error': Unknown table 'vegetables'
(DBI::DatabaseError)
```

The next section explains how to plan for and rescue
these exceptions.

```
(c)Catching Errorsrequire 'dbi'
DBI.connect('dbi:mysql:test:localhost', 'root',
  'password') do | handler |
  begin
    query = <<-QUERY
      CREATE TABLE `vegetables` (
        `ID` INT( 8 ) NOT NULL
          AUTO_INCREMENT PRIMARY KEY ,
```

```
        `type` VARCHAR( 255 ) NOT NULL ,
        `vendor` VARCHAR( 255 ) NOT NULL
   ) ENGINE = MYISAM ;
   QUERY
 handler.do(query)
rescue DBI::DatabaseError => e
 raise DBI::DatabaseError unless
 e.message.match /already exists/
end
end
```

DBI throws exceptions of type DBI::DatabaseError
when the database engine reports that something cannot be done. To use this generic exception in a meaningful way, we have to programmatically search the
error text for clues as to what might have failed. In the
preceding example, rescue is used to catch the
DBI::DatabaseError on a table creation. If the rescue
code block is entered, the variable e temporarily holds
it for us. We can then examine the error for the phrase
"already exists."

In this particular example, I am interested in ensuring
that a table already exists; perhaps this is the first time
that my *Vegetable Tracker* web application has been run
on a new server. If the text in the exception is "already
exists," we pass; otherwise, we raise the exception again
because some error *besides* the table already existing
occurred.

## 13

Working with Networking and Sockets

Ruby has a robust socket library included. This, coupled with the built-in threading, can be used to accomplish simple socket-based communications between Ruby processes or even something as significant as a web server.

For example, suppose that you implemented a library that decodes statuses and encodes commands for a Lego™ Mindstorms™ robot—as my colleague has done in a project introducing his son to programming—and you want to implement a network-controllable server for this interface, one that is sophisticated enough to handle as many as 30 students monitoring the robot. How might such a thing be done simply? Perhaps this question is most pragmatically answered by an implementation of a client-server protocol that involves exchanging Ruby objects. (Critics would be correct to point out that this would exclude participation by other software written in other languages.) Such a framework is readily facilitated by the Ruby Standard Library.

The advantages of such an approach are immediately apparent: no need to write a specification for a data format, no need to implement a stream decoder and parser, and a somewhat trivial difference between a local-only implementation and one that involves a single client to single server. The details of handling locking on the "command" aspect of a device are the only complicated component left for you, the programmer, to do. As we'll see in this section, attention should be given to both the networking-related problems in the above problem as well as the framework for passing Ruby objects (that is, Distributed Ruby).

The rest of this section details the basics of socket programming in Ruby.

Connecting to a TCP Socket

```
require 'socket'
TCPSocket.open('localhost', '80') do |socket|
  socket.print "gibberish\n"
  socket.each_line do |line|
    print line
  end
end
```

Running this script against a web server running on my own machine produces an indignant message from Apache proclaiming that my "web browser" has lost its mind. In fact, to TCPSocket, localhost might be any other machine or IP address in the world—listening on port 80 or otherwise. The protocol can be any you want to carry over the socket.

It makes more sense to read a socket in groups of bytes. This is similar to the earlier example in the section "Searching and Seeking File Contents" in Chapter 6. Here 32,768 bytes are read giving an opportunity for other threads to run:

```
while bytes = socket.recv 32768
  # handle bytes
  # give opportunity for other threads to run
end
```

Unless you are sure that the response will be short, you do not want to use #recv without a parameter. #recv will read until the socket terminates. If the response is long—perhaps megabytes—your program will hard-block until that operation finishes. As mentioned in Chapter 14, "Working with Threads," this is a symptom of Ruby not having "real" threading capabilities.

Running a TCP Server on a Socket

```
require 'socket'

server = TCPServer.new('', 10080)
puts 'Press enter to stop the server.'

# our main server connection loop
while sock_events = select([STDIN, server],
                           nil, nil)
```

```
  sock_events[0].each do |sock|
    if sock == STDIN
      puts 'Server shutdown by console input.'
      exit 1
    elsif sock == server
      Thread.new(server.accept) do |client|
        client.send 'You are '
        client.send client.peeraddr[2]
        client.send '\n'
        client.close
      end
    end
  end
end
```

In this simple example, a server is started and set to listen on port 10,080. Any incoming client is offered its
IP address or hostname immediately, in plain text.
From the client side, the output looks something like
this (telnet is a great way to debug simple socket communications):

```
$ telnet localhost 10080

Trying 127.0.0.1...

Connected to localhost.

Escape character is '^]'.

You are localhost

Connection closed by foreign host.
```

In every Ruby server approach, some method must be used to find out when a new request has arrived. Invariably, a loop structure is used to achieve this and spawn child threads to handle the incoming requests. There are two popular ways to listen for an incoming request: Either dedicate the server thread to accept only new connections (use `TCPServer#accept`, directly) or use `#select` to allow other incoming events to also be handled by the server loop. In the preceding example, I take the latter approach. Both methods block execution until *something* happens. `#select` blocks until one of the *file descriptors* given to it has something available for attention.

You don't have to use a thread to handle client communications. One approach that might be less of a headache—depending on what you are doing—would be to store all the open client connections in an array and call the `#select` method on those in turn. Something like this:

```
while events = select([server, client1,
                       client2, ...], nil, nil)
  events[0].each do |sock|

    if sock == server
      # add a new client handle to track
      # by using server.accept
    else
      # it's a client so do client stuff
    end
  end
end
```

This approach can be sufficient if communications throughput is small. In this way, you can avoid having to write complicated thread-locking semantics. However, large amounts of traffic quickly begin to choke the loop. The threaded approach would be better in the large traffic case.

Serializing Objects with YAML

```ruby
require 'yaml'
require 'socket'

matrix = [[0,1,4],
          [9,5,2],
          [3,8,7]]

TCPSocket.open('localhost', '8341') do |sock|
  sock.print matrix.to_yaml
end
```

For all but complicated, nested data types, passing the YAML (YAML Ain't Markup Language) version of data to a remote service is often the quickest and simplest way to communicate information between Ruby instances on different hosts.

In the preceding example, an array of data is sent to localhost on port 8341. On the receiver side (server), the code to receive and reconstitute a Ruby array from the YAML looks like this:

```
require 'yaml'
require 'socket'
require 'pp'

server = TCPServer.new('', '8341')

while client = server.accept
  some_obj = YAML::load client.recv(100)
  print 'Received a '
  puts some_obj.class
  pp some_obj
  client.close
end
```

This outputs the following:

```
Received a Array
[[0, 1, 4], [9, 5, 2], [3, 8, 7]]
```

Note that YAML is a pervasive standard. You can achieve cross-language message passing using this simple data format. For example, you can easily pass data from Ruby to Perl.

For efficiency, if you know both sides are the same version of Ruby, you can use Marshal instead of YAML as the conveying format. Marshal uses a binary form of the data as a storage mechanism instead of the plaintext format used by YAML.

Both forms can be written to any file descriptor, not just network sockets.

Network Objects with Distributed Ruby

```
require 'drb'

class Die
  def roll(sides)
    return rand(sides)
  end
end

mydice = Die.new
DRb.start_service('druby://:7777', mydice)
DRb.thread.join
```

Distributed Ruby is a powerful RPC mechanism—
though it does lack some features of competitors. It
provides the ability to remotely access objects running
in a different Ruby VM as though they were local. The
preceding code makes the mydice object available on
the network. To access it as a client, you might use the
following code:

```
require 'drb'

DRb.start_service
remotedice =
    DRbObject.new(nil, 'druby://localhost:7777')

puts "Remote rolled a: #{remotedice.roll(100)}"
```

When both are run, remotedice is bound to the remote
object mydice; the client sends the parameters by
Marshal, and the result is returned the same way. This
would produce the following output on the client:

```
Remote rolled a: 83
```

Using Net::HTTP

```
require 'net/http'

Net::HTTP.start('www.gnome.org') do |httpsock|
  rsp = httpsock.get('/robots.txt')
  puts rsp.body

end
```

Using Net::HTTP is trivial as can be seen in this sample.
A few attributes are available that you may also find
interesting. For example, if #code doesn't equal 200:

```
require 'net/http'

Net::HTTP.start('www.gnome.org') do |httpsock|

  rsp = httpsock.get('/foobar')

  if rsp.code != 200
      puts "Server error was: #{rsp.code}"
  end
end
```

Running this produces the following:

```
Server error was: 404
```

Using Webrick

```ruby
require 'webrick'

server = WEBrick::HTTPServer.new(
                        :Port => 1234,
                        :DocumentRoot => Dir.pwd)

class MRC_servlet <
            WEBrick::HTTPServlet::AbstractServlet
  def do_GET(request, response)
    response.body =
            '<html><body>It works!</body></html>'
  end
end

server.mount '/myrubycode', MRC_servlet

trap 'INT' do
  server.shutdown
end

server.start
```

The preceding three stanzas of code start a web server
with the current path as the root directory, establish a
URL where actual Ruby code renders a web page,
and ensure that we can shut down the web server with
Ctrl+C. Any path for which permissions are available
can be given as :DocumentRoot. Without specifying a
port number, 80 is assumed.

Actual snippets of Ruby code can handle incoming
requests by associating servlets with URLs in the server's virtual directory namespace. This is called *mounting*
and is achieved with the HTTPServer#mount method.

The inheritance of HTTPServlet::AbstractServlet provides the needed behind-the-scenes magic to make modification of the response variable sufficient.

The result is shown in Figure 13.1.

Figure 13.1   Browser rendering "It works!".

14

Working with Threads

Threading is a wonderful tool with many complications. Although cross-platform threading is not impossible, it's difficult to get right. In Ruby, the built-in threading support is implemented as Ruby threads. These threads can be expected to work exactly the same on every platform: Windows, Linux, and Mac OS X. However, you should be aware of two serious drawbacks. Ruby threads are simulated under one Ruby process, therefore:

- Multiprocessor systems will not share the load of a multithreaded Ruby application.

- If one of the pseudo-threads causes the Ruby interpreter to "block" waiting for IO, all threads will block.

The last point is likely the one you often will run headlong in to. For example, if you write a GUI application that reads data from the network and you do not make careful implementation decisions, the UI may appear to "freeze" while Ruby is waiting to read network data. Execution of your program continues when the read operation is complete; however, the freeze may lead the user to believe that your program has crashed.

At the time of this writing, in the new version of the Ruby 1.9 interpreter—YARV—that is in development, native threads from the host operating system are used. However, YARV will not benefit from the availability of more CPU processing cores due to cross-thread locking mechanisms used to avoid thread data corruption. This is the same thread synchronization mechanism used by CPython. Although there clearly is room for improvement, Ruby threading offers some benefits. (YARV stands for Yet Another Ruby VM.)

Creating a Thread

```
@return_value = 0
@magicStuff = Thread::new do
    puts 'A long process goes here.'
    sleep 5
    @return_value = 255
end
# do other stuff while other thread is running ...
# now we want to wait for the thread to finish
@magicStuff.join
puts "The return code was #{@return_value}."
```

Running the preceding code produces the following output:

```
A long process goes here.
The return code was 255.
```

In the preceding code sample, an instance of the Thread class is created using Thread::new. The code in the supplied code block executes in a private scope. That is, variables created inside the thread are local to that thread. This is where things can get tricky.

Variables in existence when the thread is created will be accessible from the outer program and also inside the thread scope. Note, however, that these are references, not copies, which means that if the main program changes a variable's value, the thread also sees this—and vice versa. See "Synchronizing Thread Communication" later in this chapter for more information. In the preceding code block, I write to the variable @return_value and then later access it from outside the private thread scope. This is possible because the @return_value variable was declared before the thread was created.

Though you do not have to, it's a good idea to always use #join to close the threads that you create to ensure that any clean-up code in your threads runs before your whole program exits.

Using a Timer

```
@pid = fork do
    puts 'A long process goes here.'
    sleep 25
    exit 255
end
@timer = Thread.new { sleep 3 }
loop do
    if Process::wait @pid, Process::WNOHANG:
        puts "The exit code was #{$?.exitstatus}."
        @timer.kill
        break
    elsif not @timer.alive?:
        puts 'Timed out; killing subprocess.'
        Process::kill 'SIGTERM', @pid
        break
```

```
    end
    sleep 1
  end
@timer.join
```

Running the preceding code sample produces:

```
A long process goes here.
Timed out; killing subprocess.
```

Here, I expand on the earlier example of creating a thread but use a child process as the item of interest. The child process to watch is created through the use of Process::fork. Using Process::fork here allows me to perform nonblocking inspection of the exit of the child process and also to have access to Process::kill when I decide that the child has been running for too long.

A Ruby library widely used for timers is called Timeout. However, it uses exception raising and rescue blocks to handle the expiration of the timer. Unfortunately, this is prone to race conditions due to the way that Ruby threads are implemented. See Ruby-talk #113417 for an in-depth explanation of why this behavior exists.

The timer implemented in the preceding code comes in two parts: the thread that expires and a loop that checks to see whether it has expired at some predetermined interval. You can use any checking interval that you want by modifying the value of the sleep argument at the end of the loop. I chose a 1-second interval because it suits this particular case well.

Although it may seem like more work to write your own examination loop, it actually ends up being rather equal work to using exception-based timers. For example, in the case where you have more than one timer running at any given time, class inheritance must be used to ensure that your rescue blocks do not accidentally rescue the wrong timer expiration. To fix this problem, we need two different exception classes that inherit from Timeout:

```ruby
require 'timeout'
include Timeout
class OuterTimeout < Timeout::Error
end
class InnerTimeout < Timeout::Error
end
begin
    timeout 10, OuterTimeout do
        begin
            loop do
                timeout 5, InnerTimeout do
                    # simulate some work
                    loop {}
                end
            end
        rescue InnerTimeout
            puts 'Inner Expired'
            retry
        end
    end
rescue OuterTimeout
    puts 'Outer Expired'
end
```

But this doesn't fix all the problems with exception-based timers. For example, what happens if a second timer expires in the middle of running the rescue block from the first timer expiration? The solution to this corner case is to have the outer and inner code block wrapped in two begin-ensure-end, respectively.

As you might imagine, the code required to do something as simple as cycle through a list of network mirrors with a cap on the total runtime of the application becomes a nightmare: seven layers of nested blocks to account for all the corner cases discussed previously. Even then, it's not 100% reliable; for example, sleep has some corner cases that do not work with the preceding code sample.

Sometimes Timeout::timeout is the right tool for the job, but you may find that you'd rather stick with a good old loop.

Killing a Thread

```ruby
@threadA = Thread::new do
    begin
        puts 'Thread A does some work.'
        sleep 5
    ensure
        puts 'Clean up code for A goes here.'
    end
end
@threadB = Thread::new do
    begin
        puts 'Thread B does some work.'
        sleep 5
    ensure
        puts 'Clean up code for B goes here.'
    end
end
@threadA.kill
@threadB.kill!
```

When run, the preceding code produces this output:

```
Thread A does some work.
Thread B does some work.
Clean up code for A goes here.
```

#kill and #exit and #kill! and #exit! are respective
co-aliases for the family of instance methods that ter-
minate a running thread. This action causes the next
scheduled thread (or main thread) in the queue to
immediately resume execution. The difference between
the two forms is simply that the latter two forms—
#kill! and #exit!—will not run the code in ensure
blocks contained within the thread being killed.

Synchronizing Thread Communication

```ruby
require 'thread'
require 'monitor'
light_switch = 0
light_switch_handle = Monitor.new
light_on_bureaucrat = Thread.new do
    100000.times do
        light_switch_handle.synchronize do
            if light_switch == 0
                light_switch += 1
            end
        end
    end
end
light_off_bureaucrat = Thread.new do
    100000.times do
        light_switch_handle.synchronize do
            if light_switch == 1
                light_switch -= 1
            end
        end
    end
end
light_on_bureaucrat.join
light_off_bureaucrat.join
puts light_switch
```

Thread synchronization is—perhaps—the most difficult and complicated of all programming problems.
Fortunately, Ruby's threading model and libraries make
it easy to solve some really common components of
this issue. In the preceding, contrived code sample, two
bureaucrats at the Office of Lightswitchery race each
other to look busy flipping the same light switch.
Admittedly, the following lines are too short to have
much of an opportunity for a race condition:

```
if light_switch == 0
    light_switch += 1
end
```

However, under the right conditions, it is conceivable
that Ruby's VM could schedule the thread out right
after the if statement and before the += assignment.
The class Monitor solves this problem. (Mutex also solves
the same problem with less overhead and features—it's
not reentrant.)

The #synchronize method ensures that the code inside
its provided block is the only concurrently running
copy of itself. In this case, both threads compete for
the lock on light_switch_handle to be allowed to exe-
cute their update code.

Additionally, Monitor has the handy capability to be
mixed in to an existing class. In so doing, this
LightSwitch class automatically gets its own
#synchronize method.

```
require 'thread'
require 'monitor'
class LightSwitch
    include MonitorMixin
```

```
    attr :state
    def initialize
        @state = 0
        super
    end
    def switch_on
        synchronize { @state += 1 }
    end
    def switch_off
        synchronize { @state -= 1 }
    end
end
light_switch = LightSwitch.new
light_on_bureaucrat = Thread.new do
    100000.times do
        if light_switch.state == 0:
            light_switch.switch_on
        end
    end
end
light_off_bureaucrat = Thread.new do
    100000.times do
        if light_switch == 1:
            light_switch.switch_off
        end
    end
end
light_on_bureaucrat.join
light_off_bureaucrat.join
puts light_switch.state
```

You can get some idea of the overhead involved in using Monitor by running the preceding code samples with and without the #synchronize method calls. You should see a large difference in run times on something this simple.

Multithreaded Exception Gathering

```
require 'thread'
class SnakeEye < Exception
end
exception_queue = Queue.new
worker = Thread.new do
    @counter = 0
    begin
        until @counter==100 do
            @counter += 1
            sleep 0.02
            if rand(6) == 0
                raise SnakeEye.new(
                "Snake Eye at #{@counter}!")
            end
        end
    rescue SnakeEye => e
        exception_queue.enq e
        retry
    end
end
while worker.alive? or
not exception_queue.empty? do
    # Check for waiting exceptions every second.
    # Report them to the user if found.
    until exception_queue.empty? do
        e = exception_queue.deq
        puts e
    end
    sleep 1
end
worker.join
```

Because it is generally considered a good idea to have only one user-interacting thread, the preceding code sample lays out a framework for collecting thread exceptions and relaying them to the main thread for display to the user. In this way, any debugging or logging faculties can be handled in a uniform fashion. In the preceding code sample, I report something similar to the following:

```
Snake Eye at 4!
Snake Eye at 9!
Snake Eye at 12!
Snake Eye at 18!
Snake Eye at 19!
(and so on)
```

The Queue class provides the synchronization. Inside the worker thread, a SnakeEye exception gets handled by the thread's own rescue block. The exception object e is then enqueued to the exception_queue. After the object is inside exception_queue, it's merely a matter of periodically checking this queue with the #empty? method.

I simply output the messages waiting to be delivered to the user, but you could also use the syslog module's debug method to log exceptions in your server-bound programs.

## 15

Documenting Your Ruby

During the 1.8 release cycle of Ruby, RDoc became the de facto documentation standard for the Ruby project, and eventually every core and standard library module's documentation was ported over to it. RDoc is now included in Ruby's standard library.

RDoc scans Ruby or C code and outputs either HTML or binary files suitable for use with the ri command. By using RDoc, your program or module can install documentation in the system, site, or user ri documentation directories just like Ruby's own included documentation.

There are other documentation options, but nothing rivals RDoc in terms of sheer market penetration. This chapter focuses exclusively on RDoc.

Documenting Ruby Code

```ruby
# This is my *Foo* class!
class Foo
    # This is my *Foo* method, *Foo#bar*
    # It does lots of interesting things to
    # instances.
    def bar
    end

    # This is my *Foo* class method, *Foo.baz*.
    # It touches class variables.
    def baz
    end
end
```

or

```ruby
=begin rdoc
This is my *Foo* class!
=end
class Foo
    =begin rdoc
    This is my *Foo* method, *Foo#bar*
    It does lots of interesting things to
    instances.
    =end
    def bar
    end

    =begin rdoc
    This is my *Foo* class method, *Foo.baz*
    It touches class variables.
    =end
    def Foo.baz
    end
end
```

Both the # style and multiline style of Ruby comment
are supported by RDoc. To make a comment private,
you can simply remove the rdoc directive from the
multiline form. For other ways of making RDoc skip
comments, see the sections "Typographic Conventions

Used" or "Hiding a Module, Class, or Method" later in the chapter.

When the preceding forms of comments are passed through RDoc, they produce documentation associated with each method, class, or module. RDoc automatically recognizes syntax conventions such as *Class.method* and *Object#method*. The next section gives more examples of special syntax, which can be used to give RDoc hints about linking and font style.

Typographic Conventions Used

```
# For emphasis, use _italic_ typeface.
# For strong statements, use *bold* typeface.
# For code samples, use +typewriter+ typeface.
#
# For <em>multi-word or multi-line</em> typeface
# changes, one can use <b>HTML-style</b> mark-up
# code: <tt>em, b and tt</tt>, respectively.
#
# \ escapes interpretation of markup
#
#--
# '--' on a line causes RDoc to ignore subsequent
# lines. These lines would be ignored.
#++
# '++' causes RDoc to continue interpretation.
# These lines would appear in documentation.
#
# Methods are referenced by their #method_name
# preceded by a # character.
#
# Internet URL's such as http://www.foobar.baz/
# are automatically hyperlinked. <IMG> tags to
# local files are also interpreted. You can also
# give a {site label}[http://foo.baz/] to a
# hyperlink. This site label replaces the URL in
# the generated HTML documentation
#
```

```
# 1. This is a numbered list.
# 2. It has a few items.
#
# * This is a bulleted list.
# * It also has a few items. "-" can be used for
#   the bullet instead of "*".
#
# a. And what list support would be complete
#    without support for alpha lists?
# b. Not RDoc, of course.
#
# [dictionaries] Lists of words with their
#    associated definitions; the "[]"s do the
#    magic. In the generated documentation, this
#    text would appear next to the word
#    "dictionaries" in a style reminiscent of a
#    standard dictionary definition.
#
# aligned dictionaries::
#    Lists of words with their definitions but the
#    output is displayed in a table-like format.
#    This is handy to help control the style of
#    the output, keeping the columns aligned.
#    Additionally, note that the indented
#    definition can start on the same line or on
#    the next line.
#
# = This would be rendered as a "Heading 1" style
# == And this would be rendered as a "Heading 2"
#    style in a smaller font than "Heading 1"
#
# --
# The above line causes a "horizontal rule" to be
# inserted in the output. Note that this is
# different from a line that starts with "#--";
# the additional space is the differentiating
# factor.
```

All of the above typographic conventions apply to C extensions as well. The only difference between Ruby code and C is that comments begin with /* and end with */; intermediate lines start with *—programmers might recognize this as the doxygen-style comment block.

Overriding Method Signatures in Documentation

```
# :call-seq:
#     width
#     height
#
# My foo method!
def foo funky_variable_names, are_here
end
```

The preceding code forces the names of parameters in the method parameter list to take on the names in the list following the :call-seq: token. So, if the override had not been used, RDoc would have generated a method signature with funky_variable_names, are_here as the parameters to the foo method. Instead, width and height are displayed as the parameters.

Additionally, the directive :yield: followed by a list forces RDoc to rename any variables yielded to associated code blocks. For example, the following code snippet would display event_to_handle as the yielded variable instead of received_event:

```
# :yield:
#     event_to_handle
#
# My listen method!
def listen &event_handler
    #... some kind of IO listener here
    yield received_event
end
```

Hiding a Module, Class, or Method

```
module Mod  # :nodoc: all
end

class Klass # :nodoc: all
end

def meth    # :nodoc:
end
```

In the preceding code :nodoc:" occurring after the #
suppresses documentation generation for each respective module, class, or method. In the case of a module
or class, you need to insert :nodoc: all.

Providing Program Usage Help

```
# This is my example program!
# It outputs a <b>Hello World</b>.
#
# Usage:
#   example.rb [--help]
#
# My licensing and copyright notification here.

require 'rdoc/usage'
require 'optparse'

user_options = OptionParser.new
user_options.on('-h', '--help') { RDoc.usage 1 }
user_options.parse ARGV

puts 'Hello World!'
```

The preceding code might be stored in a file named example.rb. When the -h parameter is passed to this program, it produces the following:

```
This is my example program! It outputs a *Hello
World*.

Usage:

    example.rb [--help]
```

If the main Ruby file of your program begins with an RDoc style comment that is separated with whitespace from any modules, classes, or methods, that comment will be output to STDOUT when the class method RDoc.usage() is called.

In the preceding example, the parameter 1 is used to cause RDoc.usage to exit with a nonzero exit code. Returning a nonzero exit code is expected when no action has been taken by the program.

To output the usage information even in cases where the options passed to the program are incorrect, use a rescue block around OptionParser#parse to cause RDoc.usage() to be called. For example:

```
begin
    user_options.parse ARGV
rescue
    RDoc.usage 1
end
```

Alternatively, RDoc.usage_no_exit() will not exit after output.

Generating HTML Documentation

```
$ rdoc
```

This is placed in a directory containing all your Ruby code, recursively. Or, for a specific file:

```
$ rdoc specific.rb
```

In the first case, the current directory is recursed to find all Ruby files and establish any relationships between files.

In both cases, documentation is output in HTML format to the doc directory in the current directory.

Generating and Installing Documentation for ri

```
$ rdoc --ri file(s)
```

This command generates the needed files for ri and places the output in your home directory under a directory named .rdoc. file can be a file or directory containing all your Ruby code; it is recursively scanned for comments.

In the case where you want the documentation installed to a systemwide directory that is protected from Linux package manager manipulation:

```
$ rdoc --ri-site file(s)
```

In both cases, the binary ri documentation format is generated and output to the directories required for ri to automatically find the documentation.

One final version is used only by someone who makes a package/tarball for a Linux distribution or an installer for another OS. The files installed by --ri-system are inserted into a directory, which is assumed to be managed by the OS package manager (that is, the contents may be overwritten during upgrades between versions of a particular piece of software that provides ri documentation).

```
$ rdoc --ri-system file(s)
```

When using ri to test your documentation, remember that ri searches for and displays information by module, class, or method name.

## 16

Working with Ruby Packages

Before RubyGems came along, module distributors were left to their own devices—many opting to utilize some variation on setup.rb and install.rb–for distributing their packages. Underpinning these are generally Rakefiles and Makefiles. For programmers coming from *nix, this is a familiar convention. However, a lot is left to the module maintainers to implement on their own. RubyGems provides an easier way.

Today we have two *complementary* packaging systems: setup.rb and RubyGems. The two systems are both important: For packages that need a commitment to security, getting security updates from your *nix distribution requires that the module has been packaged in that distribution's packaging format. For example, consider Rails.

Maybe Rails is going to run your giant, money-making, Web 2.0 site. Wouldn't it be nice if, when running security updates on your web server, Rails was included? Well, in a number of distributions it is. For example, in Debian, Rail's source tarballs are downloaded,

and setup.rb-style packaging is easily converted in to a
.deb package. (There are distributions that mash Gems
packaging and distro packaging together in an unholy
pile of mush—for example, Fedora.) Later in the section "Making Rakefile Standalone," I demonstrate how
to easily make both systems available to distributors.

On the flip side of this consideration, if you want
Win32 users to be able to easily install and update
your modules, RubyGems must be supported because
that OS does not provide a unified update system.

It is absolutely vital that you implement *both* setup.rb
and RubyGems style packaging. Implementing both is
a little more work, but it's not too imposing: You can
have both styles in the same tarball or ZIP file, and
your users can decide which style is right for them.

For this section's examples, we are packaging a simple
RSS reader based on the one from Chapter 9,
"Processing XML." It has simple dependencies, and
we'll modify it to make it suitable for use as a rudimentary "library."

```
require 'rexml/document'

##
# RSSSimple, an example
#
module RSSSimple
  ##
  # This method takes an RSS document and
  # outputs plain text with links.
  #
  def RSSSimple::prettyprint(rssdata)
    myxml = REXML::Document.new rssdata.body
    myxml.each_element('rss/channel/item') do |e|
```

```
    puts e.elements['title'].text
    puts "=> #{e.elements['link'].text}"
  end
 end
end
```

Note that I excluded packaging a C-based Ruby extension and its `extconf.rb`. While this is worthwhile, it's an expansive subject with myriad complications—far beyond the scope of this book.

Installing a Module

```
gem install rails
```

This command invokes RubyGems, fetches the latest list of packages from the online repository, fetches dependencies, and installs your module (Rails, in this case). Note that on distributions that commit to security updates for Ruby modules (for example, Debian), this command would be as follows:

```
aptitude install rails
```

RubyGems is provided by every major Linux distribution, BSD distribution, and Solaris. On a Mac, you'll need to install it from source and compile using the following:

```
ruby setup.rb
```

For Win32, you'll need to install the ZIP file from rubygems.org the same way.

You can confirm that everything is installed correctly by running this command:

```
gem spec rails
```

Removing a Module

```
gem uninstall rails
```

This removes a gem but not necessarily any of the dependencies that were brought in to support it. Those would have to be removed manually.

Searching for a Module

```
gem query --remote --name-matches foo
```

This searches the Gem source index for any modules that match the name regex. The output would resemble the following:

```
*** REMOTE GEMS ***

Bulk updating Gem source index for:
http://gems.rubyforge.org
foo (1.0)
ufooar (0.1.1.140)
```

Updating Modules

```
gem update
```

This updates all installed modules, which is usually a good idea as new versions provide bug and security fixes. You should test that the new version doesn't break your production environment before deploying it. Cleverly, until you run `gem cleanup` old versions will remain present.

Examining a Module

```
gem unpack modulename
gem fetch modulename
gem specification modulename
```

To examine the contents of a module that has already been installed, run the first command. To examine a module that hasn't been installed yet, use the second command. To examine the technical details of an installed module, run the last command.

Packaging Your Module with Hoe

```
$ sudo gem install hoe
...
$ sow rsssimple
$ mv -f rsssimple.rb rsssimple/lib/
$ cd rsssimple
$ $(EDITOR) README.txt
$ $(EDITOR) Rakefile
$ rake package
```

The preceding sequence of commands will take you from zero to fully packaged. However, before running the final command you need to do a little house-keeping. Before running rake, modify the Rakefile to resemble the following:

```
# -*- ruby -*-

require 'rubygems'
require 'hoe'
require './lib/rsssimple.rb'
```

```
Hoe.new('rsssimple', RSSSimple::VERSION) do |p|
  p.developer('Jason Clinton',
    'me@jasonclinton.com' )
  p.summary = 'Not intended for production.'
end

# vim: syntax=Ruby
```

The preceding set of actions results in the generation of a pkg directory containing both a tarball and a gem file.

Explore what other commands have been magically created for you by running the following command:

```
rake -T
```

Creating a Simple Test Case

```
require './lib/rsssimple.rb'

require 'net/http'
http = Net::HTTP.new 'www.npr.org'
http.open_timeout = 30
http.start
raise "Connection failed." unless http
response = http.get('/rss/rss.php?id=1001')
RSSSimple::prettyprint(response)
```

Placing this code in lib/test_rsssimple.rb enables a rake test rudimentary test case. When run from the top-level directory, the output resembles:

```
Woods Wins Golf's U.S. Open in 19-Hole Playoff
=> http://www.npr.org/templates/story/...
Iowa Flood a Huge Blow to Tiny Oakville
=> http://www.npr.org/templates/story/...
```

Distributing Your Module on RubyForge

```
$ rubyforge setup
$ rubyforge config
Getting jclinton
Fetching 1 projects
$ rubyforge names
groups:
packages: rsssimple
$ $(EDITOR) History.txt
$ rubyforge login
$ rake release VERSION='0.0.1'
$ rake announce
$ rake publish_docs
```

The preceding eight commands are all that are required to go from nothing to fully open source. RubyForge is generous in granting project space; if you haven't already, you'll need to apply for space. The approval process usually takes a day.

Only the last four commands need to be run to update RubyForge with any new release of your project.

The first command, setup, creates a config file and invokes your text editor so that you may supply your username and password to RubyForge.

The second command, config, fetches information about your account from RubyForge.

The third command, names, is only informative. It shows a list of projects known to RubyForge.

It's always a good idea to record notable changes that should be heeded by your end users in History.txt. The information entered here is referred to again.

login caches an authentication token with RubyForge that can be used for later uploads.

The final three commands perform the actual release.
The release commands version parameter provides a
way to do some additional sanity checking; it needs to
align with the VERSION in your project's variable declaration of VERSION included in the Rakefile. announce
creates a nice template email in email.txt that you can
use to mail your adoring fans. Finally, publish_docs
provides an rdoc-style documentation repository for
your users to browse on your RubyForge project page!

Making Rakefile Standalone

```
$:.unshift '../lib'
require 'rsssimple'
require 'rake/testtask'
require 'rake/packagetask'
require 'rake/rdoctask'
require 'rake'
require 'find'

PKG_NAME = 'rsssimple'
PKG_VERSION = RSSSimple::VERSION
PKG_FILES = []

File.open('Manifest.txt', 'r') do |file|
  file.readlines.each do |line|
    PKG_FILES << line.chomp
  end
end

Rake::RDocTask.new do |rd|
  rdoc_files = []
  Find.find('lib/') do |file|
      rdoc_files << file if file =~ /.*rb$/
  end
  rd.rdoc_files.include(rdoc_files)
  rd.options << '--all'
end

Rake::PackageTask.new(PKG_NAME, PKG_VERSION) do |p|
  p.need_tar = true
```

```
  p.package_files = PKG_FILES
end

begin
  require 'rubygems'
  require 'hoe'

  Hoe.new('rsssimple', RSSSimple::VERSION) do |p|
    p.developer('Jason Clinton',
                'me@jasonclinton.com' )
    p.summary = 'Not intended for production.'
  end
rescue LoadError
end

# vim: syntax=Ruby
```

The preceding modifications simply wrap the Rakefile that we already had in a begin/end block. This prevents Rake from failing because RubyGems is not there. In this way, we can help Linux distributors who want to package our library without depending on RubyGems.

The rest of the file is straightforward Rake syntax. I have provided a simple set of basic Rake rules to get you started: Make a tarball of the project and generate RDoc documentation. Unfortunately, Rake's features are much deeper than I have space to cover here.

After the modifications to the file are complete, two new commands become available: rake package and rake rdoc. These two commands are not dependent on the presence of RubyGems.

Index

FREE Online Edition

Your purchase of **Ruby Phrasebook** includes access to a free online edition for 45 days through the Safari Books Online subscription service. Nearly every Addison-Wesley Professional book is available online through Safari Books Online, along with over 5,000 other technical books and videos from publishers such as Cisco Press, Exam Cram, IBM Press, O'Reilly, Prentice Hall, Que, and Sams.

SAFARI BOOKS ONLINE allows you to search for a specific answer, cut and paste code, download chapters, and stay current with emerging technologies.

Activate your FREE Online Edition at www.informit.com/safarifree

> **STEP 1:** Enter the coupon code: I9EE-LEUD-79W7-7EDL-DEJ5.

> **STEP 2:** New Safari users, complete the brief registration form. Safari subscribers, just login.

If you have difficulty registering on Safari or accessing the online edition, please e-mail customer-service@safaribooksonline.com